Sexism & Misogyny

Editor: Danielle Lobban

Volume 427

First published by Independence Educational Publishers
The Studio, High Green
Great Shelford
Cambridge CB22 5EG
England

© Independence 2023

Copyright

This book is sold subject to the condition that it shall not,
by way of trade or otherwise, be lent, resold, hired out or otherwise
circulated in any form of binding or cover other than that in which it
is published without the publisher's prior consent.

Photocopy licence

The material in this book is protected by copyright. However, the
purchaser is free to make multiple copies of particular articles for instructional
purposes for immediate use within the purchasing institution.
Making copies of the entire book is not permitted.

ISBN-13: 978 1 86168 887 3

Printed in Great Britain

Zenith Print Group

Acknowledgements

The publisher is grateful for permission to reproduce the material in this book. While every care has been taken to trace and acknowledge copyright, the publisher tenders its apology for any accidental infringement or where copyright has proved untraceable. The publisher would be pleased to come to a suitable arrangement in any such case with the rightful owner.

The material reproduced in **issues** books is provided as an educational resource only. The views, opinions and information contained within reprinted material in **issues** books do not necessarily represent those of Independence Educational Publishers and its employees.

Images

Cover image courtesy of iStock. All other images courtesy of Freepik, Pixabay and Unsplash.

Additional acknowledgements

With thanks to the Independence team: Shelley Baldry, Tracy Biram, Klaudia Sommer and Jackie Staines.

Danielle Lobban

Cambridge, May 2023

Contents

Chapter 1: Sexism

There's finally an internationally agreed upon definition of sexism. Here's why that matters	1
'It's just everywhere'	3
Harmful gender stereotypes causing lower self-esteem in girls and poorer reading skills in boys, study finds	8
Jane Austen novel given 'gender stereotyping' trigger warning	10
It's time to flip the sexist script	12
Sexism: See it. Name it. Stop it.	14

Chapter 2: Misogyny

What is misogyny?	18
Men under 30 are less accepting of women's rights	21
Misogyny runs deep: how to stand up to sexist language	22
Misogyny as a hate crime – what it means and why it's needed	23
Are we at breaking point when it comes to tackling misogyny?	24
Expert opinion: misogyny against women and girls is everyone's responsibility, and government responses do not go far enough	26
What is the #MeToo movement?	28
Street harassment – it's not ok	30
Research finds that 97% of women in the UK have been sexually harassed	34
'They're desperate to be accepted': how boys as young as 14 are sucked into the world of incels	35
The draw of the 'manosphere': understanding Andrew Tate's appeal to lost men	38
Boys at Yorkshire schools idolising misogynist Andrew Tate warn headteachers as they take drastic action	40
Stopping violence against women starts with learning what misogyny really is	41
Useful Websites/Where Can I Find Help?	42
Glossary	43
Index	44

Introduction

Sexism & Misogyny is Volume 427 in the **issues** series. The aim of the series is to offer current, diverse information about important issues in our world, from a UK perspective.

About Sexism & Misogyny

With a rise in misogyny and sexist behaviour in the past couple of years, it is time that we explored the reasons behind this abhorrent behaviour. From gender stereotypes to the #metoo movement this book looks at how we can tackle sexism in all forms.

Our sources

Titles in the **issues** series are designed to function as educational resource books, providing a balanced overview of a specific subject.

The information in our books is comprised of facts, articles and opinions from many different sources, including:

- Newspaper reports and opinion pieces
- Website factsheets
- Magazine and journal articles
- Statistics and surveys
- Government reports
- Literature from special interest groups.

A note on critical evaluation

Because the information reprinted here is from a number of different sources, readers should bear in mind the origin of the text and whether the source is likely to have a particular bias when presenting information (or when conducting their research). It is hoped that, as you read about the many aspects of the issues explored in this book, you will critically evaluate the information presented.

It is important that you decide whether you are being presented with facts or opinions. Does the writer give a biased or unbiased report? If an opinion is being expressed, do you agree with the writer? Is there potential bias to the 'facts' or statistics behind an article?

Activities

Throughout this book, you will find a selection of assignments and activities designed to help you engage with the articles you have been reading and to explore your own opinions. Some tasks will take longer than others and there is a mixture of design, writing and research-based activities that you can complete alone or in a group.

Further research

At the end of each article we have listed its source and a website that you can visit if you would like to conduct your own research. Please remember to critically evaluate any sources that you consult and consider whether the information you are viewing is accurate and unbiased.

Issues Online

The **issues** series of books is complemented by our online resource, issuesonline.co.uk

On the Issues Online website you will find a wealth of information, covering over 70 topics, to support the PSHE and RSE curriculum.

Why Issues Online?

Researching a topic? Issues Online is the best place to start for...

Librarians

Issues Online is an essential tool for librarians: feel confident you are signposting safe, reliable, user-friendly online resources to students and teaching staff alike. We provide multi-user concurrent access, so no waiting around for another student to finish with a resource. Issues Online also provides FREE downloadable posters for your shelf/wall/table displays.

Teachers

Issues Online is an ideal resource for lesson planning, inspiring lively debate in class and setting lessons and homework tasks.

Our accessible, engaging content helps deepen students' knowledge, promotes critical thinking and develops independent learning skills.

Issues Online saves precious preparation time. We wade through the wealth of material on the internet to filter the best quality, most relevant and up-to-date information you need to start exploring a topic.

Our carefully selected, balanced content presents an overview and insight into each topic from a variety of sources and viewpoints.

Students

Issues Online is designed to support your studies in a broad range of topics, particularly social issues relevant to young people today.

Thousands of articles, statistics and infographs instantly available to help you with research and assignments.

With 24/7 access using the powerful Algolia search system, you can find relevant information quickly, easily and safely anytime from your laptop, tablet or smartphone, in class or at home.

Visit issuesonline.co.uk to find out more!

Chapter 1 — Sexism

There's finally an internationally agreed upon definition of sexism. Here's why that matters

We asked an expert why having a definition is such a big deal.

By Imogen Calderwood and Erica Sánchez

Europe's leading human rights organisation has just adopted the first-ever international legal instrument to stop sexism.

The Council of Europe – which includes 47 member states, 28 of which are members of the European Union – has officially recognised that sexism is 'widespread and prevalent in all sectors and all societies,' and is now calling on states to stop it.

The council adopted a recommendation to prevent and combat sexism last week.

These recommendations are essentially a list of guidelines for member states to be exploring within their own societies. They are intended as a springboard to identify and define an issue, and lay out some ideas about how member states can now be tackling those issues.

A very significant part of the recent recommendation includes what is reportedly the first-ever internationally agreed upon definition of the term 'sexism.'

And here it is! Sexism is defined as: 'Any act, gesture, visual representation, spoken or written words, practice, or behaviour based upon the idea that a person or a group of persons is inferior because of their sex, which occurs in the public or private sphere, whether online or offline.'

The recommendation also stressed that sexism is a manifestation of 'historically unequal power relations' between men and women – which leads to discrimination and prevents the full advancement of women in society.

It adds that sexism is 'widespread and prevalent in all sectors and all societies and … sexism and sexist behaviours are rooted in and reinforce gender stereotypes.'

A particularly interesting point – especially for anyone who's been accused of being 'too sensitive' when it comes to calling out everyday sexism – is that the recommendation makes the link between sexism and violence against women and girls.

Acts of everyday sexism, it says, are 'part of a continuum of violence that create a climate of intimidation, fear, discrimination, exclusion, and insecurity which limits opportunities and freedom.'

It seems a bit unbelievable that we've managed to get to 2019 without an internationally recognised definition of sexism. So we asked Jacqui Hunt, the European director of Equality Now, an NGO that works to protect the rights of women and girls, why a definition is so important.

'What's important is that this resolution recognises the issue [of sexism] is a problem in all walks of life, blocking women and girls from achieving their potential,' Hunt said. 'The definition indicates some of the impact this has on women and girls, why this is a problem, and that this has to be addressed.'

One significant advantage of having a clear definition of sexism is that it forces more general recognition that sexism is a problem, and helps explain exactly what that problem is, what causes it, and how it can be addressed.

'I think it's because we're all victims of sexism and we're all blinded by sexism,' said Hunt. 'We're all influenced by the environments in which we're brought up and if you think about it and examine it closely there's sexism all over, and you don't even realise that you're subjected.'

'We're living through these stereotypes so you don't examine how rife it is,' she added. 'So I think there has to be general recognition that this is a problem, and how stereotypes and sexism fit into that.'

'But the devil is in the detail, and until you know what it [sexism] looks like, where misogyny and sexism is all pervasive, it's difficult to understand where you could have that real focus,' added Hunt.

This is, of course, not the first time that international efforts have been made to tackle sexism and sexist behaviours. The UN's Sustainable Development Goals (SDG) are a great example of a global front in the fight.

SDG No.5 exists to tackle gender inequalities, and other issues that stem from stereotypes, lack of empowerment, and lack of inclusion, added Hunt.

'There has been growing recognition that this is an issue, and to encapsulate it and remind people [through defining the problem] is a very good way of starting to take it seriously,' continued Hunt. 'Once you recognise it and see it, it's a good springboard to take it seriously and look at how you are going to address it.'

The recommendations adopted by the Council of Europe come as a direct result of movements like #MeToo and #TimesUp, which have really shone a light on the fact that sexism is persistent and all-encompassing.

The council's Committee of Ministers have been very careful to highlight that sexism is rife in all different walks of life – from education, to advertising and media, the justice sector, culture, and sport, to name a few.

Among some of the actions included in the recommendation are legislative reforms to condemn sexism; define and criminalise sexist hate speech; and provide appropriate remedies for people who have experienced sexist behaviour.

It's not just women and girls who are negatively impacted by sexism either, of course. For example, one of the many issues highlighted in the recommendations, according to Hunt, are the unequal roles child-raising and child caring roles we have in our society.

'Sexism is very obvious in a lot of laws, for example, that child marriage is possible. That's pretty obvious,' she said. 'But then you look at things like the fact only women can claim maternity pay when they have a child. Great that they can get that, but why only women?'

'The resolution has pointed out the unequal child-raising roles and child caring roles, and so it's looking also at the family and seeing how we can balance those roles to give all parents the equal right to spend time with their children,' she continued.

Perhaps most importantly, however, is the fact that the Council of Europe represents dozens of governments, and those governments had to come together to discuss the resolution. The idea is that each of those governments will now be able to take their learnings home with them, and start addressing sexism in their own countries.

The recommendation also calls on member states to monitor their progress in implementing the guidelines, and to tell the Council of Europe's Gender Equality Commission about the measures they have taken and the progress they have achieved.

Hunt added: 'It's a growing realisation that actually our societies are embedded in sexism, and it's a very good beginning on how to address it, to then take action to move forward.'

1 April 2019

Glossary

Sexism is defined as: 'Any act, gesture, visual representation, spoken or written words, practice, or behaviour based upon the idea that a person or a group of persons is inferior because of their sex, which occurs in the public or private sphere, whether online or offline

Research

Create a survey to find out people's views on sexism. Try to ask a variety of friends and family. Do they have any experience of sexist behaviour? Is there any difference between the ages or genders? Present your findings in an infographic.

The above information is reprinted with kind permission from Global Citizen.
© 2012-2023 Global Poverty Project, Inc.

www.globalcitizen.org

'It's just everywhere'

An excerpt from *A study on sexism in schools – and how we tackle it.*

Summary

Sexual harassment

Sexual harassment is highly prevalent in schools. It is also gendered, overwhelmingly involving boys targeting girls.

- Over a third (37%) of female students at mixed-sex schools have personally experienced some form of sexual harassment at school.
- Almost a quarter (24%) of female students at mixed-sex schools have been subjected to unwanted physical touching of a sexual nature while at school.
- Almost one in three (32%) teachers in mixed-sex secondary schools witness sexual harassment in their school on at least a weekly basis. A further 36% say they witness it on a termly basis.

Sexist language

The use of misogynist language is commonplace in schools.

- 66% of female students and 37% of male students in mixed-sex sixth forms have experienced or witnessed the use of sexist language in school.
- 64% of teachers in mixed-sex secondary schools hear sexist language in school on at least a weekly basis. Over a quarter of teachers (29%) report that sexist language is a daily occurrence

Sexist stereotypes and behaviour

Gender stereotyping is a typical feature of school culture, often reinforced through mundane, 'everyday' actions.

- A quarter of all secondary school teachers say they witness gender stereotyping and discrimination in their school on a daily basis, and a further quarter say they witness it on a weekly basis.
- Over a third (34%) of primary school teachers say they witness gender stereotyping in their school on at least a weekly basis. Over half (54%) say they witness it on at least a termly basis.
- 36% of female students in mixed-sex schools say they have personally been treated differently on account of their gender, compared to 15% of male students.

Reporting and responding to sexism

Sexism and sexual harassment in schools has been normalised and is rarely reported.

- Only 14% of students who have experienced sexual harassment reported it to a teacher.
- Just 6% of students who have experienced or witnessed the use of sexist language in school reported it to a teacher.
- Over a quarter (27%) of secondary school teachers say they would not feel confident tackling a sexist incident if they experienced or witnessed it in school.

Action to tackle sexism

Schools are currently ill-prepared and ill-equipped to tackle sexism.

- Less than a quarter (22%) of female students at mixed-sex schools think their school takes sexism seriously enough.
- 78% of secondary school students are unsure or not aware of the existence of any policies and practices in their school related to preventing sexism.
- Over half (64%) of secondary school teachers are unsure or not aware of the existence of any policies and practices in their school related to preventing sexism.
- Just one in five (20%) secondary school teachers has received training in recognising and tackling sexism as part of their Initial Teacher Education.
- Only 22% of secondary school teachers have received Continuing Professional Development training in recognising and tackling sexism.
- Barriers to tackling sexism identified by teachers include an overly heavy focus on academic subjects (identified by 69% of teachers), teacher workload being too high (identified by 68% of teachers), and the failure of school leadership to prioritise tackling sexism (identified by 62% of teachers).

Introduction

Inequality between women and men is embedded throughout society. The education system is no exception. In fact, previous research suggests school is a key site where sexist attitudes and behaviours are fostered and experienced. Understanding and tackling sexism in schools is therefore critical to ensuring boys and girls can learn and live as equals – and to ending sex inequality in society as a whole.

> *SEXISM:* Prejudice, stereotyping, or discrimination, typically against women, on the basis of sex.

Sex inequality in society today

- Approximately 85,000 women are raped in England and Wales every year.
- Female MPs are outnumbered 2:1 by men in parliament.
- On average two women are killed each week by a current or former partner in England and Wales.
- Women working full-time are paid on average 14.1% less than men.
- In 2017 the BBC revealed that over the previous three years, police in England and Wales received reports of 2625 sexual offences, including 225 alleged rapes, taking place on school premises.

- 80% of boys who take maths and science GCSEs progress to a form of Level 3 core STEM qualification, yet just 33% of girls do likewise. This is despite the fact that 71.3% of girls who study STEM at GCSE achieve A*-C grades, compared to 62.4% of boys.
- Girlguiding UK found that 75% of girls and young women aged 11 to 21 report that anxiety about potentially experiencing sexual harassment affects their lives in some way.

Sexual harassment

Sexual harassment is highly prevalent in schools, and overwhelmingly involves boys targeting girls.

Sexual harassment is unwanted behaviour of a sexual nature which:

- Violates a person's dignity;
- Intimidates, degrades or humiliates someone; or
- Creates a hostile or offensive environment.

Sexual harassment can include verbal, non-verbal and physical acts – including sexual comments, taking 'up-skirt' photographs, or unwanted sexual touching. Unwanted sexual touching, wherein the target does not consent to the touching and the perpetrator does not reasonably believe they consent, constitutes sexual assault.

Reports from both students and teachers reveal that sexual harassment is prevalent in schools. For many students, it is simply the norm.

Sexual harassment in school is gendered: the majority of cases involve boys targeting girls. 37% of girls report experiencing sexual harassment, compared to 6% of boys. Female students are also significantly more likely to describe multiple incidents and more severe cases of sexual assault. They are also less likely to dismiss their experience as 'a joke'.

Sexual harassment has a detrimental impact on girls' confidence and self-worth. Both students and teachers report that as a result of sexual harassment, girls learn to 'take up less space'; to position themselves at the edges (of corridors, playgrounds and classrooms). Girls also adopt strategies to avoid being noticed and singled out for unwanted attention, even if this means they miss out on more positive attention and recognition of their achievements.

Sexual harassment

Students

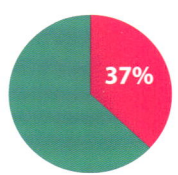

Over a third (37%) of female students at mixed-sex schools have personally experienced some form of sexual harassment at school.

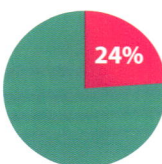

Almost a quarter (24%) of female students at mixed-sex schools have been subjected to unwanted physical touching of a sexual nature while at school.

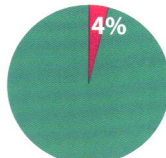

4% of male students at mixed-sex schools have experienced unwanted physical touching of a sexual nature while at school.

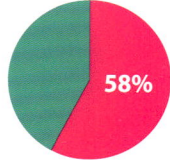

Over half (58%) of female students in mixed sex schools have experienced or witnessed sexual harassment at school.

Teachers

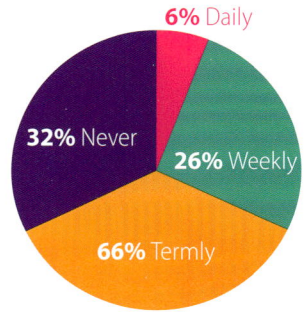

Frequency that teachers at mixed-sex secondary schools witness sexual harassment:

Almost one in three (32%) teachers in mixed-sex secondary schools witness sexual harassment in their school on at least a weekly basis.

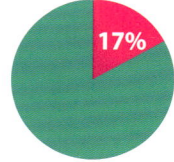

17% of primary school teachers have witnessed sexual harassment in their school.

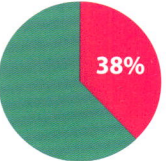

Over a third (38%) of secondary school teachers in mixed-sex schools are aware of students being sent or exposed to pornography at school.

Source: UK Feminista - "It's just everywhere" A study on sexism in schools – and how we tackle it

Sexist language

The use of sexist language is commonplace in schools.

The use of sexist, misogynist language - which denigrates girls and femaleness – is commonplace in schools.

Both male and female students report the common use of language which associates negative characteristics with being female – 'you throw like a girl', 'don't be a pussy' – and more positive characteristics with being male – 'man-up'. This language is more likely to be targeted at male students, while female students are more likely to be subjected to gendered sexual name-calling – such as 'slut', 'slag' and 'whore'.

The accepted and often casual use of language that denigrates girls/ women/femaleness fuels harmful and narrow ideas about what it means to be a man or a woman in society today. It contributes to a conducive context for sexist attitudes and behaviours – including sexual harassment.

Sexist language is also interlinked with homophobic bullying. Students and teachers in the present study report phrases such as 'that's so gay' being used by students to refer pejoratively to boys doing things stereotypically associated with girls.

MISOGYNY: Dislike of, contempt for, or ingrained prejudice against women.

Sexist stereotypes and behaviour

Gender stereotyping is a typical feature of school culture, often unconsciously reinforced through 'everyday' actions.

False beliefs and over-generalisations about differences in girls' and boys' behaviour, preferences and abilities are prevalent throughout society. Such gender stereotypes can have a deeply harmful impact on girls and boys, placing arbitrary restrictions on children's behaviour and aspirations while fuelling prejudice and discrimination.

Gender stereotyping in schools reinforces particular ideas about what is expected and acceptable behaviour from women and men: such as that women are weak and emotional, while men are strong and brave.

Sexist language

Students

Over half (54%) of female students and a third of male students (34%) say they have witnessed someone using sexist language at school.

30% of female students in mixed-sex schools have personally been described using language they felt was sexist, compared to 18% of boys.

66% of female students and 37% of male students in mixed-sex sixth forms have experienced or witnessed the use of sexist language in school.

Teachers

How frequently teachers in mixed-sex secondary schools report hearing sexist language in school:

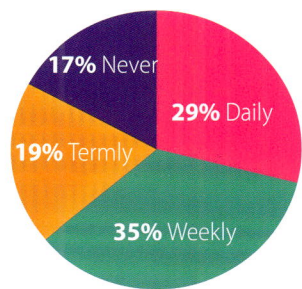

64% of teachers in mixed-sex secondary schools hear sexist language in school on at least a weekly basis. Over a quarter of teachers (29%) report sexist language is a daily occurrence.

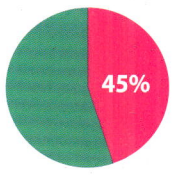

45% of primary school teachers say they are aware of sexist language being used on at least a termly basis; 15% witness it on at least a weekly basis.

Over three quarters (77%) of the examples primary school teachers gave of sexist language they heard in school involved boys using overtly female-pejorative statements such as 'don't be such a girl' and 'don't cry like a girl'.

Source: UK Feminista - "It's just everywhere" A study on sexism in schools – and how we tackle it

Sexist stereotypes and behaviour

Students

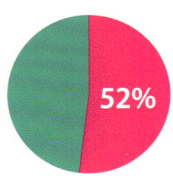

52% of female students, and a quarter of male students, say they have witnessed someone at their school being treated differently because of their gender.

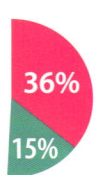

36% of female students say they have personally been treated differently on account of their gender, compared to 15% of male students.

Teachers

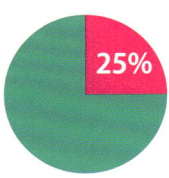

A quarter (25%) of all secondary school teachers say they witness gender stereotyping and discrimination in their school on a daily basis, and a further 26% say they witness it on a weekly basis.

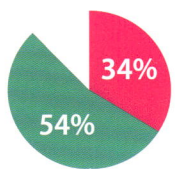

Over a third (34%) of primary school teachers say they witness gender stereotyping in their school on at least a weekly basis. Over half (54%) say they witness it on at least a termly basis.

Source: UK Feminista - "It's just everywhere" A study on sexism in schools – and how we tackle it

A significant portion of teachers report that sexism is an everyday occurrence in the classroom, and that small, seemingly insignificant events together create an environment in which pupils of both sexes come to see each other as different.

Gender stereotypes are sometimes reflected or reinforced by differential treatment in schools. The most common example students in this study gave concerned the activities that they are (or are not) allowed to participate in. Most frequently, this entails male and female students having to participate in different sports, either as a result of school policy or as a result of being excluded by other students – such as girls not being allowed to play football and rugby.

Male students are less likely than girls to express a desire to participate in sports associated with the opposite sex, but students report difficulties faced by male students who want to participate in more artistic activities, such as dance and drama.

As students progress through the school and have more opportunities to choose the subjects they study, so the influence of gender stereotypes in shaping those subject choices can be observed. This includes the stereotype that maths and science are 'boys' subjects' while art and English are 'girls' subjects'.

The resulting sex segregation within the same school is viewed by some students and teachers as inhibiting the development of equal, respectful relationships between male and female students.

Another example given by students of differential treatment concerns the tasks assigned to them by teachers. In particular, students commonly report cases of male students exclusively being asked to undertake tasks involving strength, such as moving desks and chairs or sporting equipment. Female students frequently report that they would like to be given the opportunity to do more physical tasks, and dislike being perceived as weaker than the male students.

Reporting and responding to sexism in schools

Students

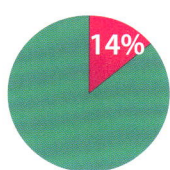

Only 14% of students who have experienced sexual harassment reported it to a teacher.

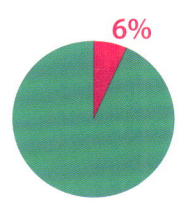

Just 6% of students who have experienced or witnessed the use of sexist language in school reported it to a teacher.

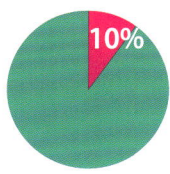

Just 10% of students who have witnessed someone being sexually harassed have reported this to a teacher.

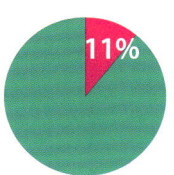

11% of female students who have been sexually harassed in school say that one of the reasons they did not report it was they felt ashamed that it happened and were scared of the consequences of reporting it.

Source: UK Feminista - "It's just everywhere" A study on sexism in schools – and how we tackle it

Teachers

Over a quarter (27%) of secondary school teachers say they would not feel confident tackling a sexist incident if they experienced or witnessed it in school.

Of the teachers who explained their reasons in the present study for not feeling confident about tackling a sexist incident, three quarters (74%) said it was because they did not think they would be supported by leaders in their school.

Reporting and responding to sexism in schools

Sexism and sexual harassment in schools has been normalised and is rarely reported by students.

The reporting of incidents of sexism and sexual harassment is crucial to providing support to those who experience it, establishing the scale of the problem, and preventing it from occurring in the future. To enable this, students need to know how and who to report incidents to, and be confident that they will be taken seriously and the report acted upon. While there are some schools doing excellent work to identify and respond to sexism, our research findings indicate that the majority of schools are not.

The main reason students give for not reporting incidents of sexism and sexual harassment is how common it is: it is seen as an everyday part of students' lives.

There is a vicious cycle of under-reporting of sexism in schools. Even when an incident occurs that students clearly recognise as harmful and unwanted, students are currently unlikely to report it. They do not believe the teacher would take reports of sexism and sexual harassment seriously, and anticipate that they would be viewed as being difficult and oversensitive.

Under-reporting contributes to a view among school leaders that sexism is not a problem requiring action – so the issue is not raised with students. This institutional silence on the matter fuels the perception (or recognition) among students that sexism and sexual harassment is considered to be 'normal' and unimportant, which in turn fuels a reluctance among students to report it.

The findings also reveal that many teachers acknowledge that even in a scenario in which they are aware of a sexist incident having taken place, they would be unclear about how to respond.

2017

Think!

Have you witnessed sexism? Have you experienced it yourself?

Make a list of sexist behaviours that you have seen in school. Consider what can be done to tackle sexism in those situations.

The above information is reprinted with kind permission from National Education Union and UK Feminista.
© 2023 UK Feminista & National Education Union

www.ukfeminista.org.uk

Harmful gender stereotypes causing lower self-esteem in girls and poorer reading skills in boys, study finds

'We need to end the "princessification" of girls and the toxification of boys,' says Fawcett Society chief executive.

By Maya Oppenheim, Women's Correspondent

Damaging stereotypes are destroying girl's self-esteem and leading to poorer reading skills among boys, a new report has found.

The study, conducted by the Commission on *Gender Stereotypes in Early Childhood*, discovered rigid gendered stereotypes are fuelling a mental health crisis among children and young people.

Researchers warned gendered pigeonholing is at 'the root' of men being substantially more likely to commit suicide than women, women being more likely to have an eating disorder, and violence against women and girls.

Three quarters of parents told the commission, which was launched by leading gender equality charity the Fawcett Society, people treat boys and girls differently from an early age. While six in 10 say this has harmful repercussions.

Parents were seven times more likely to imagine their sons working in construction and almost three times as likely to foresee their daughters becoming nurses or carers.

Sam Smethers, chief executive of the Fawcett Society, said gender stereotyping is 'everywhere' and causes 'serious, long-lasting harm'.

She added: 'From "boys will be boys" attitudes in nursery or school, to jobs for boys and jobs for girls views among some parents, these stereotypes are deeply embedded and they last a lifetime.

'We need to end the "princessification" of girls and the toxification of boys. The commercial sector too often uses gender stereotypes and segregates boys and girls simply to sell more products.

'But this is not about making everything gender-neutral. We also have to make women and girls visible when, because of pre-existing bias, the default male will still be the prevailing assumption. So for example, routinely showing children women leaders or scientists is important.'

She noted the majority of parents acknowledge there are issues around gendered stereotyping and want to eradicate this pigeonholing.

The report argues there needs to be an overhaul of education, parenting and the commercial sector as researchers warn stereotyping massively curbs career choices and drives the gender pay gap.

Professor Becky Francis, the commission's co-chair, said: 'What every parent hopes for their child, and what educators hope for children in their class, is that they will be free to achieve their potential – yet what the evidence shows is that we still limit our children based on harmful, tired gender stereotypes.

Key Facts

- Three quarters of parents said that people treat boys and girls differently.
- Stereotypes based on gender in childhood impact people throughout their lives.
- 55 per cent of black and minority ethnic (BME) staff working with children said they had witnessed black boys experiencing differential treatment based on race alongside gender.
- 49 per cent of black and minority ethnic (BME) staff working with children said they had witnessed Asian girls experiencing differential treatment based on race alongside gender.
- More than half of nursery workers, childminders, playworkers and primary school teachers working with children aged between zero and seven said they heard other members of staff say 'boys will be boys' when boys behave badly.
- One in six girls and young women in Britain has not attended school or their workplace in the past year because they were anxious about the way they look.
- Nine in ten girls said they feel a burden to tally up to an 'ideal' type of face and physique and a quarter feel 'ashamed or disgusted' by their body.

'That adds up to real harm. From boys' underachievement in reading, to the gender pay gap, the evidence is clear that the stereotypes we impart in early childhood cause significant damage to our children.

'But this is also a message of hope. If government, companies, educators and parents take action, we can challenge stereotypes and change lives, making it possible for our children to live with fewer limitations.'

Some 55 per cent of black and minority ethnic (BME) staff working with children said they had witnessed black boys experiencing differential treatment based on race alongside gender. While 49 per cent said the same for Asian girls.

More than half of nursery workers, childminders, playworkers and primary school teachers working with children aged between zero and seven said they heard other members of staff say 'boys will be boys' when boys behave badly.

A previous study, by development charity Plan International, found one in six girls and young women in Britain has not attended school or their workplace in the past year because they were anxious about the way they look.

Nine in ten girls said they feel a burden to tally up to an 'ideal' type of face and physique and a quarter feel 'ashamed or disgusted' by their body.

Researchers discovered concerns about appearance and body image were stopping girls from doing a number of important activities. Over a quarter have not left the house and a fifth have avoided public speaking due to such anxieties in the last year. One in 10 has also chosen not to take part in classes.

15 December 2020

Design

Design a poster highlighting sexist stereotypes and how to challenge them.

Brainstorm

In small groups, brainstorm gender stereotypes and make a list of those you can think of.

The above information is reprinted with kind permission from *The Independent*.
© independent.co.uk 2023

www.independent.co.uk

Jane Austen novel given 'gender stereotyping' trigger warning

University of Greenwich warns students of 'sexism' and 'toxic relationships' in Northanger Abbey, without mentioning its subtle ironies.

By Craig Simpson

Reading too many novels causes a great deal of anguish for the naive heroine of *Northanger Abbey*, and students studying the book could be similarly troubled.

This is according to academics who have issued a trigger warning for Jane Austen's work because it depicts 'gender stereotypes'.

The 1817 novel about a callow young woman's coming of age in Regency Britain has been deemed potentially upsetting by academics at the University of Greenwich.

English literature students at the university are alerted to the 'sexism' in *Northanger Abbey*, according to content notes seen by The Telegraph, and warned that the 19th-century satire contains 'toxic relationships and friendships'.

The claims are made in the content warning for Austen's work, despite the author (1775 to 1817) being widely regarded as an early feminist who rebelled against gender roles in a literary world dominated by men.

The book is taught as part of Greenwich's Gothic literature module, which itself comes with an umbrella warning that the course contains 'elements that students might find disturbing'.

Northanger Abbey tells the story of Catherine Morland, an innocent figure whose reading of Gothic novels leads her to suspect her suitor's father of being a murderous widower; a plotline intended to mock some of the macabre literature that was increasingly popular at that time.

Catherine gradually learns about the world through this ordeal, being rejected for marriage due to her lack of money by an overbearing patriarch, witnessing seducer Captain Tilney ruin her friend Isabella, and through discussions with her own love interest Henry Tilney.

She defers to him in keeping with the gender roles of 19th-century young women, as he makes observations about the sexes, including claiming of women that 'nature has given them so much, that they never find it necessary to use more than half'.

However, he also states that in matters of taste 'excellence is pretty fairly divided between the sexes'.

As narrator, Austen also wryly comments on the imbalance between men and women at the time, writing with regard to Regency romantic propriety: 'It must be very improper that a young lady should dream of a gentleman before the gentleman is first known to have dreamt of her.'

She also mocks women having to pretend to be stupid to please men, writing 'a woman especially, if she have the misfortune of knowing anything, should conceal it as well as she can.'

The fact that Austen ironically and humorously handles gender roles in *Northanger Abbey*, and her other works,

How the great Regency novelist has been dragged into the culture wars

In 2021, management of Jane Austen's House – the novelist's former home which is now a museum – said that the author's tea drinking would be subjected to 'historical interrogation' over its links to slavery.

The Hampshire museum's director argued that Austen's family was tied to the plantations due to their tea drinking, which required sugar from the Caribbean.

It was said that: 'The slave trade and the consequences of Regency-era Colonialism touched every family of means during the period. Jane Austen's family were no exception.

'As purchasers of tea, sugar and cotton they were consumers of the products of the trade, and did also have closer links via family and friends.'

In 2022, Jane Austen was replaced on a University of Stirling literature module to help 'decolonisation of the curriculum'.

The author of *Pride and Prejudice* was replaced on the Special Authors module by the African-American writer Toni Morrison.

Internal documents stated that the move would 'contribute to increased diversity' on the syllabus.

has led to claims that the Greenwich trigger warning is inappropriate.

Prof Dennis Hayes, education expert at the University of Derby and director of the campaign group Academics For Academic Freedom, said: 'Through her great wit, expressed through her characters, Jane Austen offends everyone in her novels. She is the mistress of offence. That's why we love her work.

'Students love her too. But some academics still seem to think their students are snowflakes and need coddling. How often do we have to remind them, and university management, that students are adults. They must stop infantilising them.

'Universities should put up one simple statement: Trigger warning – this is a university, you must expect to be offended.'

A Greenwich spokesman said: 'Content warnings were first used in July 2021, in response to student requests relayed to the teaching team via their student representatives during the 2020/21 academic year. It was agreed that Content Warnings should be included in reading lists so that students would be able to take them into account before encountering each text.'

30 January 2023

The above information is reprinted with kind permission from *The Telegraph*.
© Telegraph Media Group Limited 2023

www.telegraph.co.uk

It's time to flip the sexist script

Lizzie McCarthy and Sarah Davidge explain why it is vital that we recognise the role sexism and misogyny play in setting the scene for domestic abuse.

At Women's Aid we often get asked, 'why do you say domestic abuse is gendered?'

Our answer would be that even though anyone can experience domestic abuse and should have access to appropriate support, the evidence shows us that there is a disproportionate impact on women. We know that women are more likely to experience domestic abuse, are more likely to be subjected to coercive control (those abusive actions that restrict personal freedom and instil fear) and are more likely to be seriously physically and mentally harmed or killed. The kinds of support they need also tend to be very different. See the Safe blog from November 2020, Why data matters when talking about domestic abuse.

The question we ask is, why are women so much more likely to experience abuse and why is this experience so different to men?

The answer is because domestic abuse perpetrated by men against women is part of wider sexism and misogyny. It is rooted in women's unequal status in society and is part of the wider social problem of male violence against women and girls. The root causes of domestic abuse are different for women and so the responses to tackling that abuse in policy and practice have to be different too. Similarly, it is important to consider how other experiences of inequality shape survivors' experiences of abuse – including the barriers and discrimination faced by Black and minoritised survivors, LGBT+ survivors, disabled survivors and older and teen survivors.

We know from our work with survivors that sexism and misogyny permeate their experiences of domestic abuse.

Feminist writers and activists have been speaking out about harmful gendered stereotypes and their link to male violence against women and girls for decades. Women's Aid and the University of Bristol have come together to take a fresh look at this. Together, we analysed the interview transcripts of 37 survivors who had taken part in the recent ESRC (Economic and Social ResearchCouncil) funded Justice, Inequality and Gender-based Violence Project. We looked for 'gendering discourses' to see where sexism and misogyny had played a part in survivors' experiences of abuse.

Today (20th July 2021) we've published a report on the findings, *Gendered experiences of justice and domestic abuse. Evidence for policy and practice.*

We found that sexist myths which are part of everyday society had enabled and shaped the survivors' experiences of abuse. Here are three common sexist scripts that featured in survivors' experiences of abuse, with quotes from the survivors we interviewed:

1. Sexist script: Women and men should play traditional roles in the household

Flipped script: Patriarchal roles in the home can enable domestic abuse

'It really became apparent to me in … we moved in together … and it was very much … it was my job to run the household, and his to basically tell me what to do.'

'Just to be subservient and just do everything that he said and not to have a voice or an opinion,…'

'…[he] didn't lift a finger round the house but expected me to do it. I'd be called to account if things weren't done.'

'…kind of everything revolved around him…'

Survivors spoke about a hierarchy of roles in their homes or intimate relationships. For the survivors we interviewed, the man was in charge as the 'head of the household', and the woman had the unchosen role of the 'homemaker'. The survivors were tasked with household chores or running the home efficiently, without having any say in how this work was carried out. They spoke of how their male intimate partners often dictated exacting rules about how household work had to be performed, even though the men usually refused to participate in this work themselves. Male authority in the household or relationship was both underpinned and reinforced by male violence and abuse. Evan Stark in his 2007 book on Coercive Control argues that it is easier for men to coerce women through household work (rather than vice versa) because this is already socially accepted as 'women's work' (i.e. these are household roles that women are already socially expected to perform).

2. Sexist script: Women are sexual objects

Flipped script: The sexual objectification of women underpins domestic abuse

'And I think just sort of like the society that we live in at the moment it very much pushes that idea … women are objects and they're very much sexualised and … like yeah, they're there for men, like yeah there for the use of … which is … yeah that's really bad.'

The female survivors we interviewed often described themselves, and how they perceived others saw them, in terms of sexual objects. They were seen as existing for the pleasure of men and expected to engage in sexual activity that was controlled and defined by their abusive male intimate partners. The interview transcripts included reports of many offensive sexualised terms used against women ('dirty bitch', 'slag', 'slut', 'nympho') that were never applied to men. Women were seen as possessions, aggressively and jealously guarded by their male partners or 'owners'. The survivors commonly described being routinely subjected to rape and sexual coercion and harassment in their intimate relationships. It was this most intimate part of a relationship that abusive men used to cement their power and control over women.

3. Sexist script: Woman are crazy and over-emotional

Flipped script: Women are silenced with the labels of 'crazy' or 'over-emotional' when they try to talk about domestic abuse

'The courts are extremely sexist places, and there is still very much a thing about an angry loud woman is crazy, you know, and abusive men are charming … and charming with professionals.'

'…they're painting me as this crazy woman…'

The survivors we interviewed told us how labels of mental illness had long-lasting negative implications for them. Survivors themselves were seen as problematic rather than the abuse and violence committed against them being identified as the problem. This label of 'crazy' was a tool perpetrators could use to threaten survivors or call their credibility into question. Being mentally ill, or showing mental or emotional distress, seemed to be all too easily linked into wider stereotypes about women as a group being supposedly unstable, over-emotional or hysterical. Labels of being mentally unwell overshadowed many of the survivors' experiences of external responses to domestic abuse (including in court, in interactions with the police and responses from friends and family) and formed a significant barrier to accessing justice and support.

How can we flip the sexist script?

Along with our new report 'Gendered experiences of justice and domestic abuse', we have today launched a social media campaign with the hashtag #FlipTheSexistScript. It is impossible to disentangle women's experiences of domestic abuse from the violence, abuse and harassment that they are subject to elsewhere in their lives. Here's what we think needs to happen to #FlipTheSexistScript:

Specialist domestic abuse services that are run by women, for women, understand how women's experiences of abuse have been shaped by lifelong experiences of sexism and misogyny, and only they can help women truly recover from abuse. Similarly, those services that are led by and for women from minoritised groups, such as services for Black and minoritised survivors, disabled survivors and LGBT+ survivors, are often best placed to support survivors who have been subject to multiple forms of violence and oppression. They all desperately need sufficient, sustainable and long-term funding.

The root causes of domestic abuse by men against women lie in the disempowerment, objectification and silencing of women. The response must be building empowering spaces for women, challenging inequality and giving all women a voice, including women from minoritised groups. But these are under severe threat from dangerous 'gender neutral' funding approaches. You can take action to flip the sexist script by signing our petition to require local authorities to fund specific domestic abuse services for women.

Policy-makers and legislators must consistently recognise domestic abuse as a form of violence against women and girls. Unless we address inequality, we will never end domestic abuse. The Domestic Abuse Act 2021 has brought many positive changes for survivors, but in its statutory definition (the first ever statutory definition of domestic abuse) the government missed the opportunity to recognise the gendered nature of domestic abuse in law. We are also very concerned that the government is currently proposing to fragment domestic abuse from the violence against women and girls (VAWG) strategy. We strongly believe that domestic abuse must be part of single comprehensive, holistic and integrated framework to address VAWG.

Structural inequalities create power imbalances in everyday life which enable violence, abuse and harassment. To end this we all must challenge all forms of discrimination and inequality. We all need to work together to call out the sexism and misogyny that enable and entitle men to demean, objectify, abuse and control women. We need to unlearn gender stereotypes, unpick power imbalances, and unteach misogyny.

Feminist writers and activists around the time when Women's Aid began in the 1970s (and even earlier than this) warned of the harm caused by social norms about masculinity and femininity. Our research shows that these warnings remain as pertinent today as ever. It is time (in fact, it is long overdue) to recognise that until we challenge sexism and misogyny and their prominence in our society, we cannot effectively tackle domestic abuse. In other words, it's time to flip the sexist script.

20 July 2021

The above information is reprinted with kind permission from Women's Aid and thanks to Bristol University.
© 2023 Women's Aid Federation of England
Women's Aid is a registered charity in England No. 1054154

www.womensaid.org.uk

Sexism: See it. Name it. Stop it.

Sexism is any expression (act, word, image, gesture) based on the idea that some persons, most often women, are inferior because of their sex.

Sexism is harmful.

It produces feelings of worthlessness, self-censorship, changes in behaviour, and a deterioration in health.

Sexism lies at the root of gender inequality.

It affects women and girls disproportionately.

Sexism is present in all areas of life

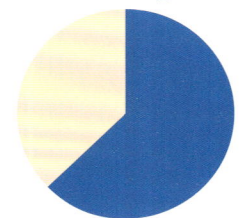

63% of women journalists have been confronted with verbal abuse

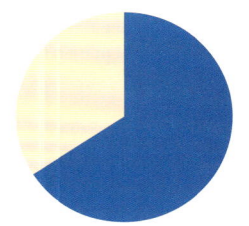

In the UK, **66%** of 16-18-year-old girls surveyed experienced or witnessed the use of sexist language at school

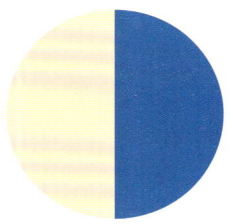

Women spend almost **twice as much** time as men on unpaid housework (OECD countries)

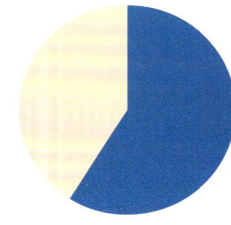

59% of women in Amsterdam reported some form of street harassment

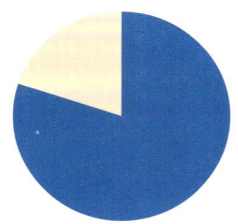

80% of women stated that they have been confronted with the phenomenon of 'mansplaining' and 'manterrupting' at work

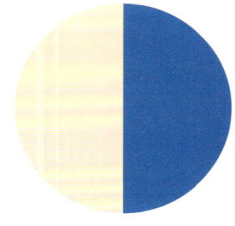

In France, **50%** of young women surveyed recently experienced injustice or humiliation because they are women

Men represent **75%** of news sources and subjects in Europe

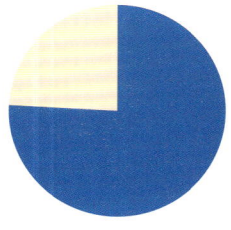

In Serbia, research indicates that **76%** of women in business are not taken as seriously as men

Source: Human Rights Channel - Council of Europe

Violence sometimes starts with a joke

Individual acts of sexism may seem benign, but they create a climate of intimidation, fear and insecurity.

This leads to the acceptance of violence, mostly against women and girls.

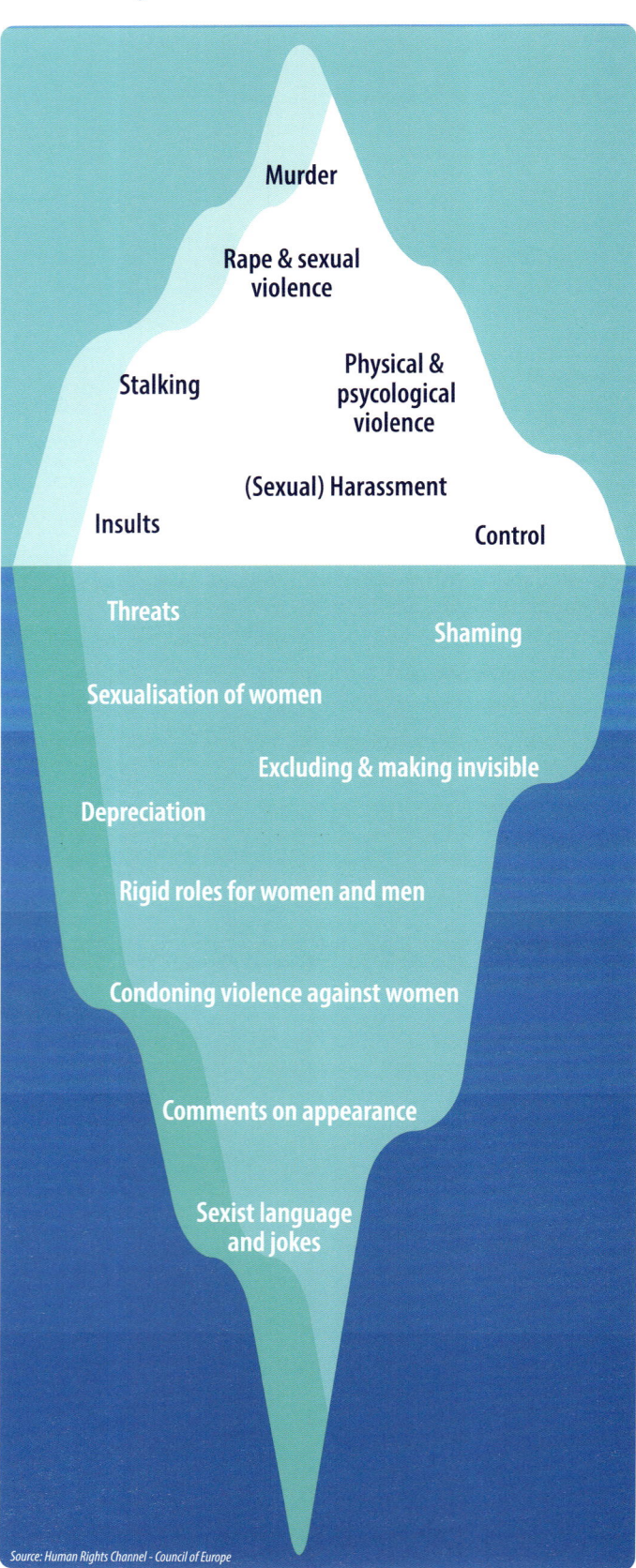

Source: Human Rights Channel - Council of Europe

issues: Sexism & Misogyny   Chapter 1: Sexism

This is why the Council of Europe has decided to act by adopting a Recommendation to prevent and combat sexism.

Sexism affects mostly women.

It can also affect men and boys when they don't conform to stereotyped gender roles.

The harmful impact of sexism can be worse for some women and men due to their ethnicity, age, disability, social origin, religion, gender identity, sexual orientation or other factors.

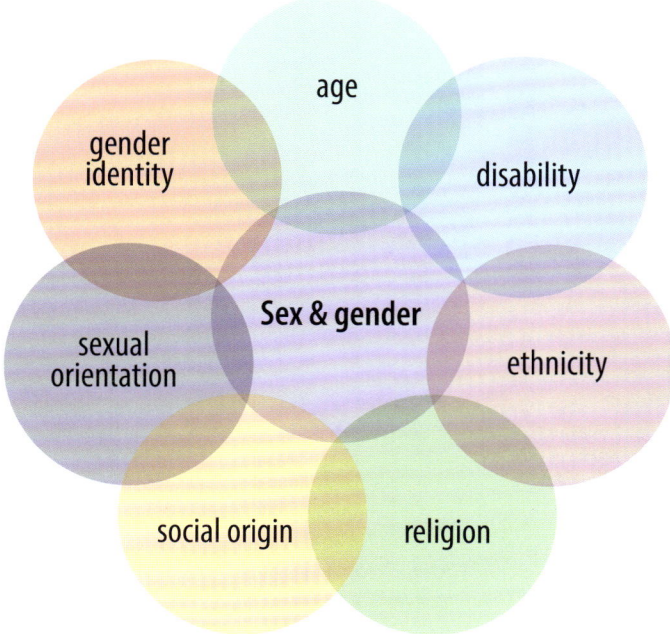

Source: Human Rights Channel - Council of Europe

Some groups of women, for example young women, politicians, journalists or public figures, are particular targets of sexism

Source: Human Rights Channel - Council of Europe

See it. Name it. Stop it.

Language and communication

Examples of sexism in language and communications:

The generic use of the masculine gender by a speaker ('he/his/him' to refer to an unspecific person). The cover of a publication depicting men only. The naming of a woman by the masculine term for her profession. A communication campaign including gratuitous nudity. An advertisement with a man showing a woman how to use a washing machine.

Why should it be addressed?

Language and communication matter because they make people visible or invisible and recognise or demean their contribution to society. Our language shapes our thought, and the way we think influences our actions. Gender-blind or discriminatory language reinforces sexist attitudes and behaviour.

How to prevent it?

Use both the feminine and the masculine when addressing a mixed audience. Review public communication to make sure it uses gender-sensitive language and imagery. Produce manuals on gender-sensitive communication for different audiences. Promote research in this area.

Media, Internet and social media

Examples of sexism in the media:

A sexualised depiction of women in the media. An all-male TV show. Media reporting on violence against women which blames the victim. Journalists, most often women, receiving comments on social media based on their appearance instead of the issues they discuss. Internet applications sending some job adverts to men only because algorithms are built in a discriminatory way.

Why should it be addressed?

Children and others are bombarded with sexist media messages and influenced by them. Such messages limit their own choices in life. They give the impression that men are the keepers of knowledge and power and that women are objects and it's ok to comment freely on their appearance. Online sexism pushes women out of online spaces. Online sexism can cause very real harm. Abusing or mocking someone online creates a permanent digital record that can be further disseminated and is difficult to erase.

How to prevent it?

Implement legislation on gender equality in media. Train media and communication professionals on gender equality. Ensure that women and men are represented in a balanced way and in diverse, non-stereotypical roles in the media. Promote advertisements that play with, and raise awareness of, gender stereotypes rather than reinforce them. Provide digital literacy training especially for young people and children. Legally define and criminalise (online) sexist hate speech. Put in place specialised services to provide advice on how to deal with online sexism.

Workplace

Examples of sexism at the workplace:

The practice of unofficially excluding women who have children from career opportunities. In meetings, ignoring

women, appropriating their contributions or silencing them. Favouring a man rather than a woman for a managerial position by presuming her lack of authority. Gratuitous comments about physical appearance or dress (which undermine women as professionals). Derogatory comments to men taking on caring roles. 'Mansplaining'.

Why should it be addressed?

Workplace sexism undermines the efficiency of victims and their sense of belonging. Silencing through sexism means that ideas or talents are ignored or under-used. Belittling comments create an intimidating/oppressive atmosphere for those confronted with them and can degenerate in violence/harassment. Victims may develop higher anxiety levels, be more prone to outbursts and depression. More generally, sexism leads to lower salaries and fewer opportunities for those confronted with it.

How to prevent it?

Adopt and implement codes of conduct defining sexist behaviour and prevent it through training. Put in place complaint mechanisms, disciplinary measures and support services. Managers must state and show their commitment to act against sexism.

Public sector

Examples of sexism in the public sector:

Sexualised comments or comments about the appearance or family situation of politicians, most often women, including within parliaments. Comments about the sexual orientation or appearance of users by staff of public services. Sexist representations / posting of images of naked women in public workplaces (e.g. hospital staff rooms). Comments on women's appearance in public spaces, including public transport.

Why should it be addressed?

The public sector has a duty to lead by example. Sexism in parliaments is very common but it limits the opportunities and freedom of women in parliaments, be they elected or staff. Sexism undermines equal access to public services. Sexism in public spaces limits women's freedom of movement. Sexism can lead to violence and creates an oppressive environment preventing mostly women from fully participating in public life.

How to prevent it?

Training of staff. Put in place codes of conduct, complaint mechanisms, disciplinary measures and support services. Implement awareness raising campaigns, such as toolkits or posters in public space explaining what sexism is. Promote gender balance in decision-making. Promote research and the gathering of data on the issue.

Justice

Examples of sexism in the justice system:

A judge implying to a victim of sexual violence that she was 'asking for it'. A law professional commenting on the appearance of a woman who is a colleague. A police officer not taking an allegation of violence against women seriously or trivialising it.

Why should it be addressed?

Such behaviour can lead to victims dropping cases. They create distrust in the justice system. They can lead to misinformed judgments. They demean women and can push them out of legal professions.

How to prevent it?

Implement policies on women's equal access to justice. Train legal and law enforcement professionals. Deconstruct judicial stereotyping through awareness-raising campaigns.

Ensure professionals base their judgments on facts, on the behaviour of the perpetrator and the context of the case rather than the victim's clothing, for example.

Education

Examples of sexism in education:

Textbooks containing stereotypical images of women/men, boys/girls. The absence of women as writers, historical or cultural figures in textbooks. Career and education counselling discouraging non-stereotypical career or study choices. Teachers making comments about the appearance of pupils/students/fellow teachers. Sexualised comments to girls. Bullying of non-conforming pupils/students by fellow pupils/students or education professionals. The absence of awareness/procedures/reactions to address such sexist behaviour.

Why should it be addressed?

The content of education and behaviour of education professionals heavily influences perceptions and behaviour. A climate of sexism in learning establishments negatively affects the achievements of pupils/students. Sexism in education can limit future individual career and lifestyle choices.

How to prevent it?

Implement policies and legislation on gender equality in education. Review textbooks to ensure that they are free of sexism and that they depict women as well as men in non-stereotypical roles. Ensure the representation of women as scientists, artists, athletes, leaders, politicians in textbooks and programmes. Teach women's history. Ensure the availability of complaint mechanisms. Teach gender equality issues as well as sexuality education (including consent and personal boundaries). Train education professionals on unconscious bias.

Culture and sport

Examples of sexism in culture and sport:

Sportswomen depicted in the media according to their family role and not their skills and strengths. Trivialising women's sporting achievements. Demeaning men who play 'feminine' sports. Women in sexy outfits as 'decoration' in cultural or sporting events. Absence of women's work in art exhibitions. Scarcity of meaningful roles for women in cinema and the virtual absence of roles for older actresses. Scarcity of funding for film production in which women have a leadership role. Under-resourcing of women's art.

Why should it be addressed?

Both culture and sport are shapers of attitudes. If women and men are depicted in stereotyped ways, this will feed into gender stereotyping. When mostly men are visible in these areas, this influences the way women are seen as potential artists or athletes and narrows the range of role models for children and young people. Gender stereotypes limit the choice of women/men girls/boys to practice sports that are not considered 'feminine' or 'masculine'; this leads to self-censorship. In both areas, sexism leads to lower salaries and fewer opportunities for those confronted with it.

How to prevent it?

Measures to encourage creative work by women and gender mainstreaming in cultural and sport policies (scholarships, exhibitions, training, provision of space/workshops). Ensure better and more media coverage of women's sports and art. Encourage sponsors to support women's arts and sports. Adopt codes of conduct to prevent sexist behaviour, including provision for disciplinary action in sports federations. Encourage leading sport and cultural figures to speak up against sexism and implement campaigns to denounce violence in sport and sexist hate speech.

Private sphere

Examples of sexism in the private sphere:

Women performing more unpaid (care and household) work than men, for example only women helping to wash dishes at a dinner party. Sexist jokes between friends. Systematically offering 'feminine' or 'masculine' toys to girls/boys. Boys being encouraged to run and take risks and girls to be docile and compliant. The use of expressions like 'running like a girl' or 'boys will be boys'.

Why should it be addressed?

Unpaid work weighs on women's participation in the labour market, on their economic independence as well as on their participation in sport and leisure activities. Toys (e.g. a mini kitchen or a construction game) influence gender roles, but also future study or career choices. Sexist jokes can intimidate and silence people and they trivialise sexist behaviour.

How to prevent it?

Awareness-raising measures and research on the impact and the sharing of unpaid work between women and men. Measures for reconciling private and working life for all. Promotion of non-gendered toys. Encouraging boys as well as girls to participate in household tasks. Giving girls, too, the space and freedom to play, explore and be themselves.

Key Facts

- Sexism affects women and girls disproportionately.
- 63% of women journalists have been confronted with verbal abuse
- Women spend almost twice as much time as men on unpaid housework (OECD countries)
- 80% of women stated that they have been confronted with the phenomenon of 'mansplaining' and 'manterrupting' at work
- Men represent 75% of news sources and subjects in Europe
- In the UK, 66% of 16-18-year-old girls surveyed experienced or witnessed the use of sexist language at school
- 59% of women in Amsterdam reported some form of street harassment
- In France, 50% of young women surveyed recently experienced injustice or humiliation because they are women
- In Serbia, research indicates that 76% of women in business are not taken as seriously as men

The above information is adapted from *Sexism: See it. Name it. Stop it.* Reprinted with kind permission from Council of Europe.
© 2023 Council of Europe

www.human-rights-channel.coe.int

Misogyny

What is misogyny?

By Krystal Jagoo

Misogyny is often conflated with sexism, or the hatred of and discrimination against women. It is a term often used to describe extreme acts of violence against women.

Words often evolve as culture shifts, though. That was the case in 2012 with Julia Gillard's speech in Parliament while serving as the Prime Minister of Australia, when she called out the Leader of the Opposition's behaviour as misogynistic.

Australia's Macquarie Dictionary even expanded its definition of misogyny to refer to an entrenched prejudice against women following this event.

A 2015 study analysed 216 articles that were published in the Australian print media in the week following Gillard's speech to explore how this accusation of misogyny was dismissed, minimized, and undermined, and found that 'these predominant constructions not only serve to maintain and justify gender inequalities, but also function to reproduce and perpetuate them.'

As this incident and the subsequent research demonstrates, misogyny devastatingly places women in an ideological dilemma: Women face challenges when making attempts to address misogyny but also deal with obstacles by ignoring misogyny, as doing so can allow misogynistic views and behaviour to be perpetuated.

How to recognize misogyny

Sometimes misogyny is overt and obvious, but it can also be covert and insidious. Some signs of misogynistic behaviour and attitudes include:

- Expressing hatred for women
- Catcalling or harassing women
- Favouring men at the expense of women
- Strong belief in rigid, traditional gender roles
- No respect or regard for women's time and effort
- Ignoring or speaking over women
- Rejecting women's ideas
- Stealing ideas from women but refusing to credit them
- Frequently interrupting women when they are speaking
- Blaming women for conflict and expecting women to maintain social harmony
- Punishing women for calling out discrimination and sexism

The above are examples of misogyny, but it is important to remember that this is just a small sample of how these attitudes are expressed. While such behaviours are often displayed by men, internalized misogyny also often leads other women to participate in these behaviours as well.

The logic of misogyny

In her book, *Down Girl: The Logic of Misogyny*, Kate Manne outlines how misogyny operates to reinforce male dominance through references to the violence of Elliot Rodger in California in May 2014 and Purvi Patel's sentencing of 20 years in 2015 for feticide in Indiana.

Such examples demonstrate why folx who do not conform to societal gender hierarchies are at particular risk of harm from misogyny, given how their existence disrupts patriarchal systems.

> **Sexism vs. Misogyny**
>
> Manne differentiates between sexism and misogyny, explaining that 'sexism is taken to be the branch of patriarchal ideology that justifies and rationalizes a patriarchal social order, while misogyny is the system that polices and enforces its governing norms and expectations.'
>
> In other words, sexism justifies the patriarchal order, whereas misogyny involves the norms and expectations that help enforce it.

Women deal with the harms of misogyny perpetrated by men. After confronting these oppressive attitudes and actions, women may, in turn, internalize these beliefs.

This means that men are not the only ones to perpetuate misogynistic beliefs. Women who help reinforce the status quo are rewarded, while women who challenge or threaten it are punished.

This internalization can then contribute to their own policing of themselves and other marginalised genders to avoid becoming the victims of misogynistic violence from men.

Causes of misogyny

Misogyny is an attitude that develops due to experiences, upbringing, social influences, and cultural norms. Some factors that contribute to causing misogyny include:

- Experiences: Observing misogynistic behaviour during childhood, benefits from such beliefs, having misogynistic role models, and holding other beliefs aligned with misogyny can all play a part.

- Upbringing: Growing up in a household and being exposed to forms of misogyny is often a critical factor in the development of such attitudes. Researchers have also shown that childhood exposure to domestic violence and emotional abuse is associated with sexism, misogyny, and violence towards women.

- Cultural factors: Cultural attitudes about women can also play a role. Religious attitudes, which may suggest that women are inferior, subservient, or sinful, can contribute to contempt and mistreatment.

Impact of misogyny

Evidence suggests that misogyny can have a serious impact on mental health and well-being. One study found that women who experienced sex discrimination had:

- An increased risk of developing clinical depression
- More psychological distress
- Worse mental functioning
- Poorer self-rated health
- Lower life satisfaction

Women are also more likely to experience a number of different mental health conditions, including anxiety, depression, PTSD, and eating disorders. Some of these differences may be linked to biological differences. However, the disparity is likely influenced by factors such as exposure to chronic stress and trauma caused by sexism, discrimination, misogyny, and gender inequality.

> Sexist microaggressions have been linked to anxiety, depression, anger, and low self-esteem, and prolonged exposure is associated with trauma symptoms.

Online misogyny in the headlines

When misogyny is perpetuated via social media and other online platforms, it can produce dangerous outcomes.

#GamerGate

According to a 2015 journal article, #GamerGate refers to a number of incidents that followed a blog post by Eron Gjoni on August 8, 2014, in which he wrongly accused his ex Zoe Quinn of sleeping with a game critic for a positive review of her game Depression Quest.

His accusations resulted in online and offline harassment of this woman, as her home address and phone number were publicized, and she received rape and death threats. The #GamerGate harassment campaign quickly expanded to other prominent women in the video game industry, including Brianna Wu and Anita Sarkeesian.

> The violent consequences of online harassment extend far beyond the digital spaces in which they may begin. Several critics of #GamerGate were 'swatted,' meaning that strangers made fraudulent calls to the police and sent SWAT teams to the critics' houses.

A 2018 journal article reviewed how misogyny is particularly prevalent online and aligns with other oppressive practices, including white supremacy, queer antagonism, ableism, etc.

Based on data from 2017, the Pew Research Center found that attitudes towards online harassment vary by gender, as 70% of women felt that this was 'a major problem,' while only 54% of men felt that way, and 63% of women felt that it was more important to feel safe online than be able to share opinions freely, while only 43% of men felt that way.

> **Experiences and attitudes reinforce misogyny**
>
> When marginalised genders who suffer the harms of misogyny are up against men who minimize the issue of online harassment in favour of free speech, such violations are likely to continue.

Types of misogyny

A few different types of misogyny have also been identified.

Misogynoir

> **Misogynoir:**
>
> Misogynoir is a specific subtype of misogyny that involves contempt and prejudice directed specifically against Black women.

In 2018, Moya Bailey and Trudy, the Black women who had substantial roles in defining misogynoir and championing the term, described it as 'the anti-Black racist misogyny that Black women experience' and discussed how misogynoir operated to erase their work itself.

By this, despite their success in shedding light on the phenomenon of misogynoir, it continues to operate to harm these Black women. Unfortunately, marginalised genders who are also oppressed in other ways, such as being Black and queer, continue to be at greater risk of harm by misogyny, given how they challenge gender hierarchies.

To illustrate misogynoir at work, Manne delved into the Daniel Holtzclaw case 'of the serial rapist police officer in Oklahoma City, who preyed on Black women who had criminal records, in the belief that these women would have no legal recourse.'

In this way, anti-Black misogyny was perpetrated against these Black women long after his acts of sexual violence towards them through descriptions of him in articles and documentaries that promoted him as incapable of such violations by loved ones, doubts of Black folx as credible witnesses, etc.

> Unfortunately, Black women continue to face further risks of being harmed by misogyny due to how it aligns with anti-Blackness, and they confront additional roadblocks when attempting to get justice.

Transmisogyny

> **Transmisogyny:**
>
> Transmisogyny refers to prejudice, hatred, and oppression directed toward transgender women and transfeminine people. It describes the intersection of misogyny and transphobia.

A 2018 study conducted by a queer Japanese American social worker on trans feminine adults in New York City found that 'participants highlighted their victimization experiences as involving misogynistic attitudes and behaviours combined with transphobic exhibitions of devaluation, fetishisation, and objectification.'

As this qualitative research demonstrates, trans women of colour are at heightened risk of being harmed by transphobia, misogyny, and white supremacy. All of these intersecting threats contribute to:

- Underemployment
- Poverty
- Housing concerns
- Health challenges
- Legal issues
- Victimization

Tips to deal with misogyny

Dealing with misogyny is not easy, but some strategies may help. Steps you can take to care for yourself and others who are faced with misogynistic behaviour include:

- Don't ignore it: Call out misogynistic behaviour when you see it and make it clear that it is not acceptable.
- Report it: In work settings, talk to your manager or human resources department.
- Leave the situation: Setting boundaries can be helpful, but it is often best to leave the situation if possible.
- Create safe spaces: Support and uplift all women. Work to become more aware of the damaging effects of internalized misogyny and how it can lead to the punishment of women who challenge the patriarchal status quo.
- Care for yourself: Practice self-care and relaxation strategies to deal with stress.

If misogyny is causing distress or disruptions in your life, you may also find it helpful to talk to a mental health professional. They can help you process your experience, develop new coping strategies, and explore ideas for how to deal with misogynistic behaviour.

A word from Verywell

Despite the pervasive harms of misogyny, as reviewed here, you may find that folx are hesitant to address it directly, even when in positions of relative privilege, such as a wealthy white cisgender woman, which is part of how this oppressive system continues to be perpetuated.

Ultimately, you may need to reflect on your own unique needs and the challenges involved, when confronted with it, as those who have opposed misogyny often deal with overwhelming backlash as a result.

Unfortunately, while it is understandable why folx may be apprehensive of directly opposing misogyny, especially given how it can impact mental health negatively, such avoidance only contributes to further harms to the most vulnerable of marginalised identities, such as Black trans women, whose high risk of being murdered is due to the harsh reality of transmisogynistic violence that still disproportionately harms them.

29 September 2022

Published with permission from Verywell Mind, Dotdash Meredith. All rights reserved
© 2023 Dotdash Media, Inc.

www.verywellmind.com

Men under 30 are less accepting of women's rights

Study finds young men see themselves as being in competition with the opposite sex.

By Gabriella Swerling, social affairs editor

Men under 30 are less accepting of women's rights than their older counterparts, a new study suggests.

The EU-wide study suggests that while Western democracies have become increasingly gender-equal over the past decades, there is a more recent 'backlash against gender equality in the form of rising modern sexism'.

Furthermore, young men are more likely to see women's progress at their expense and the trend is most prominent in areas with high unemployment and less trust in institutions, according to the findings.

Researchers from the Department of Political Science at Sweden's Gothenburg University, found that young men see themselves as being in competition with women.

Gefjon Off, a PhD student, who worked on the research, said: 'Some people believe that increased gender equality only benefits women and do not see the benefits for society as a whole.

'Some research suggests that this feeling of injustice can even motivate citizens to vote for right-wing radical parties who are against feminism and sexual freedom.'

Impact on political attitudes and voting behaviour

Previous research has shown how a perceived sense of injustice and competition between men and women affects political attitudes and voting behaviour.

The current study, published in the journal Frontiers in Political Science, surveyed 32,469 people across the EU's 27 countries.

Respondents were asked to state to what extent they agree with the statement that promoting women's and girls' rights has gone too far because it threatens men's and boys' opportunities.

'The results show that young men aged 18 to 29 most often agree with this statement in our survey,' Ms Off added.

'The older the men are, the less they agree with this statement. Some women agree with the statement, but to a far lesser extent than men of all ages.

'The results contradict previous research claiming that the older generation are the ones who are the most conservative and opposed to advances in women's rights.'

Ms Off added: 'Possibly, young men who believe that women are outcompeting them in the labour market experience advances in women's rights as unjust and a threat.

'We need to get better at communicating the benefits of gender equality. Fathers get to spend more time with their children and the burden of being the family's breadwinner is lightened when mothers in families also advance in their careers.'

Slovak men oppose advances in women's rights

The survey also found that Slovakia is the EU country in the study where the highest proportion of young men are opposed to advances in women's rights. In some regions there, unemployment has risen by as much as 1.1 per cent in the last two years.

The study also shows the inverse situation. In regions such as northern Italy where unemployment has fallen and where social institutions are perceived as reasonably impartial, young men are less resistant to advances in women's rights.

In Sweden, the largest proportion of young men who agree with the survey statement that advances in women's rights threaten men's and boys' opportunities live in regions where unemployment has risen in the last two years.

Professor Nicholas Charron, who also worked on the study, said: 'More than other EU citizens, Slovaks think that their own country's public institutions are not impartial, that is, that their social institutions favour certain groups of people.'

He added: 'The gap between young women's and young men's views on advancing women's rights is great in Sweden, among the top 10 in the EU according to our measurements.'

The fact that young men stand out in this context may be due to their position on the labour market. At a young age they may not yet have a stable job, or they may not have progressed as far in their careers as older men.

The rise of 'incel culture'

This study comes amid the global rise of 'incel' culture, referring to 'involuntarily celibates' who discuss their resentment and hatred of women, and are often unable to get a romantic or sexual partner despite desiring one.

Last year, 22-year-old Jake Davison shot and killed five people in Plymouth, before turning the gun on himself. He was interested in incel culture and considered them as 'people similar to me'.

More recently, Andrew Tate, the controversial influencer, whose videos have been banned and condemned for extreme misogyny, has been associated with fuelling the internet phenomenon.

2 October 2022

The above information is reprinted with kind permission from *The Telegraph*.
© Telegraph Media Group Limited YEAR OF PUBLICATION

www.telegraph.co.uk

Misogyny runs deep: how to stand up to sexist language

Our journey as feminists means we are constantly learning; and sometimes this means learning to unlearn language we previously accepted, or at least tolerated. It means learning to challenge that language. This blog aims to provide feminist readers with some tools to help build confidence in how we address sexist language in our own lives and interactions.

By Clemmy Manzo

All too often we hear sexist remarks about women and girls, which are then passed off as casual jokes. Worse still, this exposure to sexist language starts young: in the UK, 66% of 16-18-year-old girls have experienced sexist language at school. It's a global issue, and one that continues into adulthood. Women in high-ranking positions are not spared sexism either: in Africa, for example, a total of 67% of the women parliamentarians interviewed reported being repeatedly subject to sexist remarks and attitudes over the course of their parliamentary mandates.

Language matters. It even shapes the values of a society. It's therefore important to understand that sexist language is part of the patriarchal system and a culture of misogyny that harms women. If, as a society, we accept and allow sexist language, we're sending a message that it's OK to demean women, and if it's OK to demean women, then it's not too big a leap to see how harassment and verbal abuse might feel OK to some. So the next time someone says their sexist language is 'just a joke', know that this isn't acceptable at all.

The diagram below helps visualise how sexist talk and rape culture are intrinsically linked. Sexism, objectification, and the restrictive nature of traditional gender roles all feed into a culture of misogyny that create a barrier to women achieving equality – and perpetuate violence. And when we consider that 1 in 3 women across the globe experience violence in their lifetime, we see how vital it is to challenge sexism in all its forms.

'Individual acts of sexism may seem benign, but they create a climate of intimidation, fear and insecurity. This leads to the acceptance of violence, mostly against women and girls.' – The Council of Europe

So how can you challenge sexist language, without feeling like a killjoy or, worse, exposing yourself to risk?

The first thing to do is to champion non-gendered language in your everyday vocabulary. Stay away from words that perpetuate stereotypes or strip women of their power.

And then there are some useful tactics that you can use for calling out sexism directly:

- Don't validate a sexist comment with a laugh. By laughing, you're saying 'this is OK with me.'
- Don't just let it pass. It's not always easy to say something, but if it's safe to do so, challenge the use of sexist language.
- Ask questions. What did they mean by that? Was it funny? Why did they feel the need to refer to the person's gender?
- Remind them of their better self. Would they have said that if they were in a different setting?
- Or express outright disapproval. 'I didn't like what you said and I don't think it's funny.'
- Know your boundaries. If this turns into a debate, recognise your own limits and don't feel guilty for shutting down the conversation.

It's worth practising some of these tactics to yourself out loud, and on friends. You'll find it easier to incorporate them into your life if you've tried them out first.

Finally, if you witness someone challenging this language, support them – be an ally. And if you're the one being challenged on your language, don't get defensive. Listen. Learn. In order to challenge the current culture of misogyny, we must work together and be willing to do better.

31 March 2022

The above information is reprinted with kind permission from Womankind.
© Womankind 2023
www.womankind.org.uk

Source: An Empirical Exploration Into the Measurement of Rape Culture (Nicole Johnson, Dawn M. Johnson)

Misogyny as a hate crime – what it means and why it's needed

By Felicia Willow

Recently, the government announced that it will instruct all police forces across the UK to start recording crimes motivated by sex or gender on an experimental basis – effectively making misogyny a hate crime. This follows the example of Nottinghamshire Police in 2016, followed by another 10 police forces since.

Classing misogyny as a category of hate crime would not make anything illegal that isn't already. The law has not changed – it is solely about how we record these crimes.

The Fawcett Society – the UK's leading membership charity campaigning for gender equality – celebrated this as a victory, after years of campaigning for this result. We have taken action such as calling on police chiefs to make misogyny a hate crime nationwide, revealing data that gender is the most common basis for hate crime attacks on women, supporting the recent bill heading to the House of Lords, contributing to the Law Commission consultation on the subject, and launching a MP letter writing campaign to support the change.

The murder of Sarah Everard was a terrible event that pushed this campaign onto the national stage. Nearly 6,500 people wrote to their MPs through our online tool, and protests and vigils across the country sent a message to the government that it was time to act.

The days that followed brought forward thousands of stories from women across the country, sharing their experiences of harassment, assault, not being believed, and constant fear. It has also raised the stories of Black women including Nicole Smallwood, Bibaa Henry and Blessing Olusegun who, unlike Sarah, did not receive the public attention that they should have, highlighting that we as a society have a long way to go on both sexism and racism.

Misogyny is a major issue, but we cannot ignore racism and the intersecting experiences of different groups of women when we fight against it.

Making misogyny a hate crime is, at face value, about collecting and processing information.

But, it could be so much more than that.

This decision sends a message that sexism and misogyny are not acceptable. That this behaviour is on a level with other hate crimes such as racism, Islamophobia, anti-semitism, homophobia, transphobia, and ableism.

But we also need to move towards a better understanding of how protected characteristics intersect. Women experiencing, for example, harassment for wearing a hijab are experiencing both Islamophobia and misogyny. We need to gain a better understanding of this – amongst our police and in our society.

We live in a country where sexism is accepted. Where women are constantly subjected to inappropriate behaviour that is seen as the entitled right of men.

This sexism was no more obvious than in the reaction to the decision. People – mainly a certain kind of man – howled in protest:

'Does that mean we can't wolf-whistle anymore?'

'Mother-in-law jokes are out!'

'It's political correctness gone mad'.

This attitude demonstrates how widely accepted the belief is that men are more entitled to behave misogynistically than women are entitled not to be treated hatefully.

Violent crimes against women in our society are not taking place in an otherwise equal world. They are built on and held up by locker room banter, rape jokes, 'give us a smile', cat-calling and, yes, even mother-in-law jokes.

Until we have a world that respects women, we need to recognise this behaviour for what it is – the basis on which violent crimes in our society are not only committed, but carried out largely with impunity and a lack of adequate response from police.

Making misogyny a hate crime sends a message to our society, to our police and to our criminal justice system that enough is enough. Women deserve respect and attacks against us motivated by our sex or gender must be taken seriously.

5 August 2021

The above information is reprinted with kind permission from Family Law.
© 2023 LexisNexis

www.familylaw.co.uk

Are we at breaking point when it comes to tackling misogyny?

By Rebecca McQuillan

Every so often, I find myself comparing notes with other women about sexual abuse. I often wonder how many have experienced it.

Among those I've spoken to, the tally is 100 per cent.

The abuse they describe ranges from unpleasant comments, up to and including rape; usually, people relate multiple incidents. Crude comments, groping, men exposing themselves, men threatening them, being followed in the street: these things are, or have been, part of the tableau of their lives.

The implicit threat of abuse or violence creates cordons round women's lives. It's second nature to women to be vigilant. Out for a walk up a hill with my husband at night recently, we were struck by the number of men we passed, the dark evenings no impediment to them getting some exercise.

We passed no women. No evening run for them. Perhaps it seems obvious to point this out, but it's the very ordinariness of women's fear that is so shocking.

Attitudes were more openly sexist in the 1990s and before, as women who came of age then will remember.

But we'd be kidding ourselves to imagine that younger women are strangers to sexual assault and harassment. The internet provides a new manifestation of an old problem by giving boys and young men access to misogynist influencers and pornography, some of it violent.

A UK poll by the children's charity Plan International found that more than half of girls had experienced sexual harassment at their school, college or university. Separately, it found that more than a third of girls had received unwanted sexual attention, like being groped, stared at or wolf-whistled, while wearing their school uniform in public.

According to Public Health Scotland, 10 per cent of women and two per cent of men in Scotland have been raped since the age of 13.

For all the fanfare around zero tolerance of sexual violence, you can't help but ask yourself: are we actually getting anywhere? Because sexual violence is horrendously prevalent.

Now we find out that the Metropolitan Police has had a serial rapist in its ranks for years.

David Carrick admitted this week to 24 charges of rape and 25 other mostly sexual offences against 12 women going back two decades. Many of the rapes involved violence.

'As time went on, the severity of his offending intensified as he became emboldened, thinking he would get away with it,' said Jaswant Narwal, chief crown prosecutor.

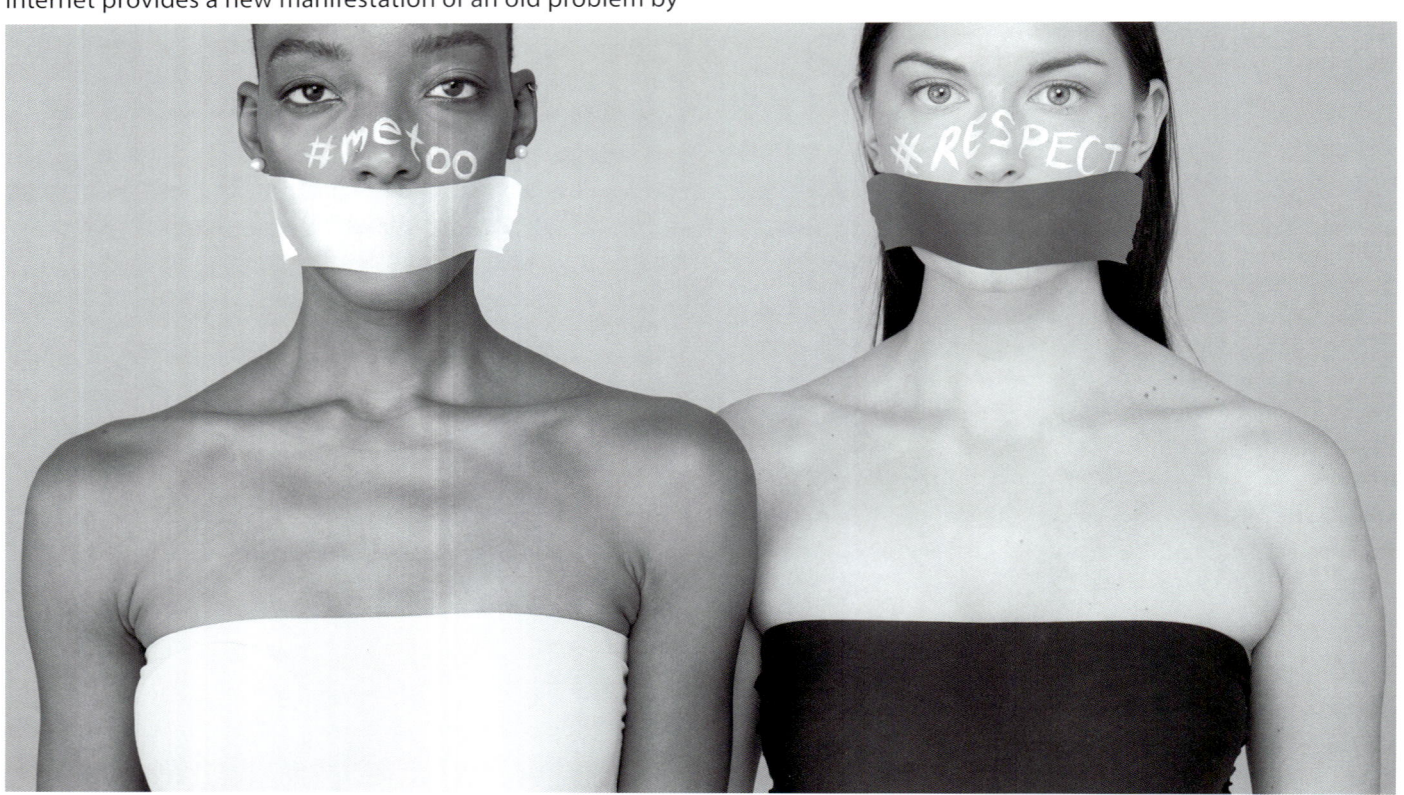

Nine separate allegations, including of rape, had been made against him to the police, but they had failed to join the dots.

As if that weren't crushing enough, 800 further London officers are being investigated over 1000 complaints of sexual and domestic abuse.

I'd call it unbelievable except it isn't. The horrific murder of Sarah Everard by a serving Met officer in 2021 had already peeled back the lid on misogyny in the London force. Two officers were sacked in 2021 for sharing pictures on WhatsApp of the bodies of sisters Bibaa Henry and Nicole Smallman who were found dead in a north London park. Bibaa and Nicole were targeted by their killer simply for being women.

The officers referred to them as 'dead birds'.

Last year, the Independent Office for Police Conduct (IOPC) found 'disgraceful' misogyny, discrimination and sexual harassment at the Met, centred on constables at Charing Cross police station.

Now this. The Home Secretary warned yesterday that there are likely to be more shocking cases of corrupt officers to come.

We could call this a crisis for policing, which it is. But if we only see it in those narrow terms, we're missing the point. Improving vetting and misconduct procedures won't solve this alone, because the root of the problem is societal misogyny. It originates with the way men and boys are brought up to think about females.

The good news is that a lot is being done to change attitudes. In 2023, children's TV drama, books and schooling are heavily focused on respect. Primary school children as young as eight can talk the language of anti-discrimination and gender equality, and describe what that looks like.

But out of school, some children see a different set of values. As boys grow up, they can easily come across men on the internet who will tell them males are 'naturally' dominant, that they should embrace misogyny and that sex is their right to claim.

At the same time, in the last seven years we've seen a willingness for high profile public figures to break faith with the equality agenda, especially in the US. The election of US president in Donald Trump has been followed by the US Supreme Court's overturning of abortion rights.

Feminists have never taken progress for granted, but in recent years have been asking themselves: are we at crunch point? Extreme manifestations of the incel (involuntary celibate) ideology, and the popularity of internet saddos like Andrew Tate, point to a reactionary backlash with reach. The abysmal conviction rate for rape and sexual assault meanwhile make some men feel they can abuse with impunity, as the David Carrick case underlines.

We're fighting millennia of ingrained discrimination; we're wrestling with the fact that in some people, civilisation is a thin veneer.

But we can also remind ourselves of this: ultimately, David Carrick was wrong to think he could get away with it. Ultimately, he was brought to justice and stands disgraced before the world, thanks to those brave women who turned their trauma into triumph.

We've come a long way. Yes, there are vocal misogynists in the world, but they are outnumbered by vocal male supporters of women's rights. Men in 2023 now call out toxic attitudes in other men, to an extent probably never seen before. Girls grow up believing they do not have to put up with discrimination. The tide of history is flowing in their direction. The rage of the misogynists is the rage of the losing side.

But the prevalence of abuse and the lack of justice for most women who are raped or sexually abused shows starkly that the fight has only just begun.

18 January 2023

The above information is reprinted with kind permission from The Herald.
© 2001-2023 Newsquest Media Group Ltd

www.heraldscotland.com

Expert opinion: misogyny against women and girls is everyone's responsibility, and government responses do not go far enough

There has been an outpouring of grief, anger and further sharing of stories by women expressing how they feel unsafe in public spaces due to harassment by men in the aftermath of the abduction and murder of Sarah Everard. Associate Professor Loretta Trickett, Nottingham Law School, and Professor Louise Mullany, University of Nottingham, discuss what this tells us about women's safety in our current society.

The resurgence of the 'Reclaim the Night' marches, not just this weekend but over the last few years, and the #metoo movement tells us that women have had enough. We still live in a society where women are routinely harassed in public spaces by strangers who feel entitled to sexually objectify them and make them feel unsafe. The latest UN Women UK study found that 98% of all young women had been subject to harassment. This accords directly with our own research evaluation of the then 'controversial' misogyny hate crime policy brought in by Nottinghamshire Police, where gendered targeting was deemed to be prejudicial and the detrimental impact on both individual women and the wider impact on women as a social group directly paralleled racial and religious hate crime.

Despite this misogyny hate crime policy being rolled out by a growing number of police forces, and the reading of the Domestic Abuse Bill in the House of Lords, there is still yet to be a change at a national level. The policy was initially ridiculed by some sections of the mass media as a waste of police time. The same sentiments were expressed by senior policing leaders who resisted a national roll out of the policy because they had more 'serious' matters to attend. Recent violent scenes at the Sarah Everard vigil in Clapham Common have only served eroded trust in the police further. Contrary to the public and police trivialisation, the misogyny policy includes behaviours that are already criminal, including public order, physical assaults and battery, stalking and sexual assaults but which had remained largely hidden from statistics because women are unwilling to report.

Our research found that 93.7% of women had experienced street harassment, 74.9% of women reported that the incident had a long-term impact on them and 63.1% of women changed their behaviour as a consequence of the harassment and abuse. Our respondents reported feelings of intimidation and living in fear of what may happen to them in public spaces. 87.1% of members of public in our research thought the policy should be rolled out nationally. Women also spoke about a wide range of practices they use to avoid street harassment and sexual assault including carrying of keys, avoiding public transport, not exercising in public, fear of going out alone or at night – many of which have been aired as everyday universal experiences of women in the UK in the days since Sarah's disappearance.

Our findings recognised that we need to stop getting women to change and regulate their behaviour and instead include men as part of the solution rather than simply 'the problem'. The vast majority of men do not harass or sexually assault women and are appalled by this behaviour. We need these men as allies, both in calling for change and in its implementation. Many men who took part in our research were genuinely shocked by the scale and impact of a practice on women and girls that is outside of their own experiences. They are committed to helping change practices that they themselves find offensive and see the need to drive this process of social and cultural change.

Since 2018, we have continually argued for the launch of educational campaigns that place men at the centre of the discussion. As part of this, we have launched a graphic storybook to be used in schools, colleges and universities which documents the scale and impact of everyday street harassment on women and girls, how it is perceived by them and how it feeds their fear of rape and restricts their freedom of movement.

We need to educate the younger and upcoming generation of men and boys from an early age by teaching respect for women and outlining what sexual harassment and abuse looks like and what the consequences might be, embedding such learning within the mainstream educational curriculum. We need to get men involved in challenging these behaviours and working with women to provide a safer and more egalitarian society. We must make absolutely clear the differences in the masculinities of those men who respect women and those that do not whilst condemning much more loudly those who harass, exploit, rape and murder women using tougher sentences and policies.

Despite overwhelming evidence of the unacceptable levels of street harassment and gender-based violence provided from multiple sources, commitments from the government to bring in any change have been incredibly slow. There have been a handful of tokenistic gestures from PM Boris Johnson to attempt to reassure women in the wake of Sarah Everard's murder, but these do not begin to go anywhere near far enough – for a start, they ignore the culture of toxic masculinity that is endemic in everyday UK culture. The suggestion of putting plain clothes officers into nightclubs to protect women depends partly on trust in the police, which is at a particular low point. It also implies that men cannot help themselves due to presumably 'biological' urges that are beyond their control; getting men centrally involved to change the culture of other men is part of what is being ignored here.

The key issue is about tackling the attitudes of those who abuse women and girls and ensuring that they are dealt with through criminal justice measures where possible, and men educating other men is a critical part of this change. The Law Commission recommended a national roll-out of sex/gender as a hate crime as part of their consultation last year in September 2020 following a lengthy eighteen-month consultation period – surely now is the time to act on this and bring this legal change into being.

It's now five years since Nottinghamshire Police brought in the misogyny hate crime policy, and in that time many hundreds of women have been killed at the hands of gender-based violence in the UK alone, not to mention the countless numbers who have suffered emotional and physical abuse daily, all of which has been made worse by the conditions created by during lockdowns and tier restrictions. Making misogyny a hate crime and bringing about a change in the law sends a very clear message that society is at last committed to a change that is long overdue.

To ensure that the death of Sarah does not simply become another footnote in the litany of violence against women and girls, we need to dismantle the institutional and cultural sexism that enables such violence to flourish. It is time to address this in the House of Lords and for our politicians to finally take account of the significant need to show women that they take this seriously and will bring in a change in the law.

16 March 2021

Key Facts

- 98% of young women in the UK have been subject to harassment.
- 93.7% of women had experienced street harassment.
- 74.9% of women reported that the incident had a long-term impact on them and 63.1% of women changed their behaviour as a consequence of the harassment and abuse.

The above information is reprinted with kind permission from Nottingham Trent University.
© 2023 Nottingham Trent University

www.ntu.ac.uk

What is the #MeToo movement?

By Sherri Gordon

If you use social media, you've probably seen the hashtag #MeToo on Twitter, Facebook, Instagram, and other sites. What started out as a way for survivors of sexual harassment, sexual assault, and sexual bullying to bond and share their stories has become a global movement that has sparked significant changes, both social and legal.

What's more, the movement has allowed survivors to feel supported while simultaneously initiating a national–and worldwide–conversation about the widespread issues surrounding harassment, assault, and the changes that need to be made.

History behind the movement

Tarana Burke, an advocate for women in New York, coined the #MeToo phrase in 2006. She aimed to empower women who had endured sexual violence by letting them know that they were not alone–that other women had suffered the same experience.

> *Time* magazine named Burke as their Person of the Year for 2017, and she's earned the Ridenhour Prize for Courage. Today, as senior director at Girls for Gender Equity in Brooklyn, Burke speaks at events across the country.

In 2017, the New York Times published an article accusing Harvey Weinstein of sexual harassment. Actors Ashley Judd and Rose McGowan were fearlessly vocal about Weinstein's actions, which empowered many others to share their stories.

In the meantime, actor Alyssa Milano embraced the #MeToo hashtag across her social media. She'd been unaware of the phrase's origins and how quickly it would catch on, thinking of it as a simple way to create awareness, find support, and build a community of survivors.

Impact of the #MeToo movement

After Milano's tweet, Twitter users posted the hashtag almost a million times within two days, according to Twitter. The movement spilled over to Facebook, too, where about 4.7 million users shared 12 million posts in fewer than 24 hours. Years later, people continue to share their stories with the hashtag #MeToo across social media platforms.

The response was especially meaningful for people who worked with survivors of sexual assault and harassment on a daily basis, Finally, the issue they had been working tirelessly to address was gaining traction and garnering worldwide attention. The local grassroots effort Burke spearheaded had now expanded to reach a community of survivors from all walks of life.

> In the wake of these disclosures, many prominent people in entertainment, sports, and politics have been exposed for sexually harassing or assaulting others.

Thus, the silence surrounding sexual harassment and assault is being broken. Many are now open to and passionate about discussing the issues. The #MeToo movement has prompted sweeping changes, such as:

- Affirmed for survivors that they are not alone
- Developed a stronger community where survivors have a voice
- Demonstrated how widespread the issue is
- Shifted social norms and opinions about the issue
- Exposed belief systems that enable abuse
- Increased compassion for survivors
- Updated and enacted laws and policies
- Created avenues for survivors to speak up and share their stories
- Broke the silence surrounding sexual harassment, sexual assault, and sexual bullying
- Destigmatised the issue and made it safe for discussions
- Punished many powerful men through legal action and negative public opinion
- Highlighted the need for formal anti-harassment policies
- Prompted several states to ban non-disclosure agreements, which help powerful people hide their actions by buying survivors' silence
- Created the Time's Up Legal Defense Fund, which has provided legal representation to thousands of survivors
- Resulted in new legal standards by the International Labour Organization

Sexual harassment and assault statistics

The issue of sexual aggression is pervasive. Nationwide, 81% of women and 43% of men reported experiencing some form of sexual harassment or assault, according to a 2018 study conducted by the University of California and the non-profit Stop Street Harassment.

Although the #MeToo movement has accomplished a great deal in little time, some advocates aren't as optimistic about the successes. The issue is still on the public's radar, but sexual assault continues. It's particularly insidious for people who are transgender, Native American women, college students, members of the military, and people of colour. Women remain at a higher risk for sexual assault than men.

Harassment and assault can be devastating, often leading to substance use, suicide, psychiatric disorders such as PTSD, and other negative outcomes.

What's next for #MeToo?

Although positive change continues, much work remains to be done.

For example, survivors of sexual assault and harassment still endure victim-blaming, not to mention the threat of retaliation for speaking up. People need education on how perpetrators set up situations to their advantage, sometimes groom their victims, and often get away with harassment and assault.

A prime example is actor Bill Cosby's 2021 release from prison after a Pennsylvania court threw out his conviction for sexual assault, despite ample evidence. He was among the first wave of prominent people to be tried and convicted of such crimes.

A word from Verywell

Today, the phrase #MeToo is still a sign of solidarity for victims of sexual harassment and assault. Tweets, Facebook posts, and Instagram posts featuring the hashtag #MeToo still appear daily–evidence that the #MeToo movement has created awareness and a community of support.

Still, there is so much to be addressed, from changes in federal laws to real safety for survivors who speak up. Society might never be completely rid of this scourge, but efforts continue to uncover such crimes, encourage reporting without retribution, and bring the perpetrators to justice.

24 April 2022

Published with permission from Verywell Mind, Dotdash Meredith. All rights reserved
© 2023 Dotdash Media, Inc.
www.verywellmind.com

Street harassment – it's not ok

An excerpt from the report *Street harassment – it's not ok: Girls' experiences and views.*

By Jessica Southgate and Lucy Russell

What is street harassment?

'Street harassment' is generally understood as an umbrella term that describes unwanted and face-to-face sexual attention from strangers in public spaces that is targeted at girls and women by boys and men who they don't know. Bristol Zero Tolerance, for example, describe a set of behaviours that encompasses a wide range of possible gender-based harassment, including for trans, non-binary and gender-fluid young people:

'Unwanted comments, gestures, and actions forced on a stranger in a public place without their consent and directed at them because of their real or perceived gender (whether male, female or non-binary).'

Street harassment, therefore, can include unwanted whistling, staring, comments, shouts, sexual name-calling, persistently talking to someone, or asking for their name and phone number, even when they have said no. It can include being photographed, filming, upskirting, being followed, flashing, public masturbation, groping, sexual assault, rape and hate crimes.

Plan International UK commonly heard that harassment happened to girls in a number of locations, throughout the day and in different parts of their lives. As one from the participants in the Nottingham Women's Centre 'Because I am a Woman' film says, '... the thing about street harassment is that it doesn't have a particular place or a particular time – it's happening everywhere and anywhere and at any given time and place'.

Street harassment is a type of sexual harassment, and as such should be seen as a form of gender-based violence. Understanding these behaviours as being part of the continuum of violence against women and girls is a theory first set out by Professor Liz Kelly. It is a useful lens to understand how different forms of sexual violence are connected. It describes how violence such as rape, sexual assault and sexual harassment of all kinds is underpinned by social norms of entitlement that allow and encourage these behaviours to be directed (primarily by boys and men) towards girls and women. Thinking in this way 'enables the linking of the more common, everyday abuses women experience with the less common experiences labelled as crimes'.

Some people have suggested that the phrase 'street harassment' is too narrow and fails to capture a range of other types of harassment that can be experienced in public places, for example, harassment on public transport, taxis, online, or in clubs or bars. It might also miss out other types of unwanted behaviours that do not appear to be direct harassment, such as comments like 'Cheer up luv'. It also does not explicitly reference that it is gendered power dynamics at play, leading academic Dr Fiona Vera-Gray to suggest that 'men's stranger intrusions on women in public space' may be one term that could capture this range of harassment types.

Although the majority of the incidents described to us came from strangers directed towards the girls, other incidents, such as being catcalled or surrounded by a group, could also come from people they knew, for example, boys from their school. Girls themselves often do not distinguish between the harassment they experience in these spaces, and through the focus groups we ran for this report, harassment in a number of different types of spaces was raised. Online, in the street, or at school, harassment clearly impacts on girls' lives and limits their freedom. The frequency and pernicious nature of the harassment, combined with limited adult reactions, sends a message that sexual harassment should be tolerated as part of daily life.

> **'I feel like it's [Street Harassment] also part of the 'bro culture' isn't it?...**
>
> **My dad says, 'You know what men are like.' It's like, yeah I do but also like, I'm not going to like stop living.'**
>
> Thea, 18, London

Given the benefit that having a widely understood term brings and the opportunities this provides to continue to build an international solidarity movement, 'street harassment' remains a helpful and appropriate term. We use this term throughout this report to refer to all types of sexual harassment in public spaces, including public transport and public social places like bars and clubs.

We recognise that while the majority of girls experience street harassment, not all girls will experience harassment in the same way. Through this report, we aim to emphasise the gendered nature of such harassment and highlight how it intersects with other identity factors, profoundly changing how it feels to the person experiencing it. We look at how experiences of harassment in public overlap with harassment in schools, colleges and universities, however we do not address how this extends to the workplace as this was outside the scope of this project.

There is no source of national UK data that can give an accurate picture of the extent of the problem as it affects girls, so the picture we build has been drawn from a number of different sources. Data that can be disaggregated by gender, age and other identity characteristics that would reveal to what degree girls experience harassment in public, for example on the way to school or when travelling on the bus, does not exist. We recommend that any further work to challenge public harassment must address these gaps as a matter of priority.

Gender and public space

The ways in which boys and young men experience, use and think about public space is likely to be very different from girls and young women. Research in Amsterdam, for example, into girls' and boys' use of public playgrounds (one of the first public spaces children learn to negotiate) observed that girls were marginalised, assuming the status of a 'minority group', and that boys outnumbered girls in how frequently and how long they participated and in the 'network and territory they controlled'. In research led by Professor Emma Renold, girls described widespread gender-based harassment, entrenched sexism and 'banter' which impacted negatively on their well-being and freedom of movement. One 13-year-old girl gave an example, saying 'boys older than me like whistle at you and like stare at you and like wink at you and like shout, "Oi, you over there" or something,' while another girl (also aged 13) said '[t]here's these little kids on the bus... pointing at me saying oh that girl has big tits.'

Boys, in contrast, can experience other types of threat and intimidation in public space, as seen in some of the harms facing young people, through serious youth violence and gangs. Death and injury from knife crime tends to affect young men in particular, for example. The most common reason given by young men for committing a violent offence is self-defence and this is also the reason most frequently given for carrying a knife, suggesting that some young men can feel a profound sense of threat and potential harm in certain public spaces. What can also be overlooked, however, is that girls in these contexts face specific gendered threats, such as being exposed to violence and sexual exploitation through gangs.

Other personal characteristics, including age, ethnicity, faith, gender identity, disability and social location, also impact

66%
of girls in the uk have experienced sexual attention or sexual or physical contact in a public place

38%
of girls experience verbal harassment like catcalling, wolf-whistling and sexual comments at least once a month

One analysis found that nearly all victims were female and all but two perpetrators were male

63%
of young adult women (aged 18 to 24) had experienced inappropriate sexual behaviour in night-time venues

35%
of girls wearing school uniform have been sexually harassed in public

More than
1 in 3
girls in the uk have received unwanted sexual attention such as being groped, stared at, catcalled and wolf-whistled while wearing their school uniform in public

1 in 8
girls said their first experience of unwanted sexual attention or contact in a public place was when they were 12 years old or younger

1 in 7
girls have been followed while in uniform

42%
of 14 to 21-year old bame women reported unwanted sexual attention at least once a month

49%
of LGBTIQ+ young women and people experienced unwanted sexual attention at least once a month

London was rated 9th worst of 15 of the world's largest capitals in terms of women reporting public transport to be safe

22%
of women in the uk reported some experience of sexual touching, groping, flashing, sexual assault or rape while they were in or around school

66%
of victims of reported sex offences on school premises are girls or women, with 94% of alleged perpetrators men or boys

Source: Street Harassment It's Not OK - Girls' experiences and views (Plan International UK)

on young people's experiences of public space. Whilst most boys are much less likely than girls to experience sexual harassment in public, gay, bisexual, trans or non-binary boys can also be victims of harassment, with sexual harassment often intersecting with homophobia, biphobia and transphobia. Stonewall reports that three in ten LGBTIQ+ people (29 per cent) and more than two in five trans people (44 per cent) avoid certain streets because they don't feel safe there. Whilst we have focused specifically on girls in this report, addressing the discriminatory attitudes that underpin gender-based harassment of all lesbian, bisexual, trans and intersex (LGBTIQ+) young people must go hand in hand with efforts to tackle the harassment of girls.

Girls that Plan International UK spoke to for this report thought that there were considerable differences in how boys and men thought and behaved, and remarked that it would be unlikely for women to harass other people because they understood what it felt like to be on the receiving end. They also thought that a girl harassing a boy would be unlikely to cause fear, and there was amusement at how unlikely that behaviour would be: *'I think if a girl went up to a boy and asked about his colour underwear and squeezed his bum people would be like: "What are you doing?!"'* – Nyasha, 14, Belfast

As the girls we spoke to identified, young women are socialised to think constantly about their own safety and take personal responsibility for staying safe frequently by restricting their access to public places. In the UK, girls are significantly more worried than boys about being followed by a stranger (34 per cent of girls compared to 19 per cent of boys), with catcalling and other forms of street harassment highlighted as major crime and safety issues by girls.

Girls we spoke to felt that boys were much less likely to be brought up with the same considerations about their own personal safety. They were also unlikely to understand how their behaviour might affect girls or impact on the choices girls make about where they go or what they do. As Sam, 22, said: *'It wouldn't affect them so why would it affect a girl?'*; and Grace, 18, commented: *'Men will never know how scary it can be – they will never know what it's like to be afraid of walking down the street at night.'*

This report shows that sexual harassment (in all the spaces where they experience it) has a profound effect on how girls form their identities and learn to take up space in the world. As one youth worker said: *'When you're younger you're trying to come up with your identity. You then question yourself more: am I too sexy, am I wearing the right clothes? It's just another confusion – to suddenly be sexualised at a time when you're also developing physically. It can be really confusing.'* – Amanda, 46, youth worker, Manchester

The journey to fully eliminating street harassment is likely to be a long one, involving significant shifts in attitudes and overall increases in gender equality in all its forms.

As Superintendent Ricky Twyford, who was involved in the original Project Guardian to tackle unwanted sexual behaviour on London transport, said: *'This is going to be a constant cycle of work to eradicate the wider problem of misogyny that has existed for a long time – the battle to address it is going to be a long one.'*

With the current high profile of the #MeToo movement and a strong call for women's experiences of sexual harassment to be understood and their stories listened to, now is a key opportunity to make girls' voices heard and create the change they too want to see.

Types of harassment of girls

'Catcalling'

The behaviour most commonly reported by the girls Plan International UK spoke to was being shouted at or 'catcalled'. This is demonstrated elsewhere, for example with 65 per cent of girls in one survey in Wales saying sexual harassment was one of the main issues they faced, and that 'catcalling' and using words like 'slut', 'slag' and 'whore' were common amongst their peers.

Girls described the fear, shock and shame catcalling caused them, and the impact this had on where they went and what they felt free to do. Being shouted or beeped at by men in moving vehicles was seen as a particular problem, with girls describing an acute sense of being singled out, drawn attention to and wanting 'to be swallowed up' when this happened. Not being clear about who the person was, whether they knew them or knowing how to respond made these experiences worse.

Unwanted touching and physical harassment

Girls frequently experienced unwanted touching or invasions of their personal space which went unchallenged. Girls also described behaviours that may not be categorised as criminal but which were often experienced as intimidating. The feeling of being 'stared at' was commonly identified, for example, and led to similar feelings as catcalling – shame, embarrassment and wanting to 'disappear'. Hair, whether afro, redhead or dyed bright colours, was described as being a particular entry point for men feeling entitled to speak to girls or touch them.

Girls described acts that were experienced as threatening and intimidating, like people getting too close, interrupting them or making an excuse to touch them, for example putting their hands on their waist to move past them in a doorway. These sorts of behaviours could be read either as unwelcome over-familiarity or deliberate intimidation, for example when groups of boys or men lined a path or blocked a doorway. Importantly, the frequency of such behaviours means that they should not be seen as isolated small incidents but instead they need to be viewed for their cumulative impact.

A small but worrying number of girls in focus groups reported incidents of more serious physical and sexual harassment, including being grabbed and groped. A number talked about incidents that happened on nights out, including being groped in a queue and being pinned up against a wall on a night out. These types of experiences are also commonly reported elsewhere. The case studies highlighted in this report add to the reports of physical and sexual assaults. One Drinkaware survey found almost two-thirds (63 per cent) of young adult women (aged 18 to 24) had experienced inappropriate sexual behaviour in night-time venues; 76 per cent felt disgusted and 71 per cent felt angry as a result.

One girl described an incident of having been grabbed by a man when she was out shopping with her mum.

'I was at an ATM with my mum... I remember it so clearly, we were shopping, and a guy came along and whispered in my ear: "It's national grab an arse day", and he grabbed me... I was 15, with my mum, doing Christmas shopping. People always say "keep yourself safe, don't wear this, don't go to these places" but like how possibly could I have avoided that? Don't go outside!?' – Lucy-Anne, 19, Belfast

One girl, for example, described having had witnessed a man masturbating in front of her. Whilst this was not a common occurrence described in focus groups, these kind of sexual acts, including men exposing themselves, are often named in apps and online reporting platforms such as Hollaback! on which women can record harassment experiences. This kind of offence has also been reported by academics:

'[Flashing and public masturbation is] a huge and common experience for girls in adolescence who are under 18.' – Dr Fiona Vera-Gray

Crime survey figures for England and Wales show an increase in adult victims of sexual assaults in part due to overall improved reporting from women who are victims of indecent exposure or unwanted sexual touching.

Girls in school uniform

Girls frequently described witnessing and experiencing harassment at a very young age, sometimes as young as eight years old. In all of the cases described, girls felt sure that the age of the girls being targeted must have been clear to the harasser, particularly when the girls were in school uniform or travelling around school time. They were shocked that this did not appear to stop men from harassing and commented on how badly the harassment could affect them.

A survey by Plan International UK has found that 35 per cent of girls wearing school uniform have been sexually harassed in public. More than a third of girls in the UK have received unwanted sexual attention such as being groped, stared at, catcalled and wolf-whistled while wearing their school uniform in public. The survey also found that one in seven girls had been followed while in uniform, eight per cent said they had been filmed or photographed by a stranger without their permission or someone had taken a photograph up their school skirt (known as upskirting). One in eight girls said their first experience of unwanted sexual attention or contact in a public place was when they were 12 years old or younger.

'I can remember walking down a road in Sheffield with my sister and her friend and they were about ten at the time and some older man wound his window down and whistled at them and it just made me feel sick – like how can you not see they're children?' – Natasha, 25, youth worker, Sheffield

Girls described what they saw as the sexualisation of young girls in the minds of adults, identifying a clear parallel between girls reaching puberty, developing physically and the attention they received from men. Some said that looking older as a young woman was 'worse'. Those who described themselves as 'developing early' in particular talked about both unwanted sexual attention from strangers and sexual bullying in the classroom, and the fear and intimidation this could cause.

'I think as soon as a pair of tits are in their [a boy's] face, that's it.' - Sarah, 21, Sheffield

'I used to be quite breasty, I used to have the horns beeped at me two three times a day.' – Rachel, 23, Manchester

Those who were slightly older often reflected back on how much worse the harassment had been when they were younger or talked about having witnessed the harassment of younger girls and how shocking and distressing they found it.

'Young girls especially, who are already under pressure, or who are developing boobs and have their period and they feel like little girls, and then suddenly they're sexualised – which is completely new to them – it's a really scary situation for them.' – Georgia, 20, Manchester

Concerningly, girls felt that being in school uniform made them a particular target. They described feeling sexualised and fetishised by 'older men targeting school girls'. Data gathered through the Bristol Street Harassment Project survey found 58 per cent of people had first experienced harassment when they were between 10-15 years old, with one saying: 'First time I was harassed on the street, I was 13 and in my school uniform during secondary school. I was walking home and around three older men on the other side of the road whistled at me.' Similarly, staff from the Angelou Centre (for BAME women) reported girls not wanting to go anywhere after school as they were sexually harassed and approached in the street by adult men they did not know when in uniform.

'To be perfectly blunt, it was the fetishism of school uniform, school girls. And you're like, I literally just come out of a six-hour day at school, can you please not? I have other things to worry about – but that is what it is. That school girl thing. It definitely is a thing... It's the whole like, you know that Robin Thicke song "she's a good girl", "Blurred Lines" – it's like "she won't do anything either because she's a good girl". It's a really warped pervy old man thing. But that is something you have to be aware of.' – Lucy-Anne, 19, Belfast

Despite being on their way to or from school, girls clearly did not feel safe and were extremely self-conscious about their uniform and how much of a 'target' they felt it made them.

'I've never experienced harassment like I did then [at school]. Men would ask if they could take a picture with me in my uniform. It was awful. Before that I used to be walking home, and I was so scared walking home.' – Ffion, 25, Edinburgh

2018

*Names have been changed

The above information is reprinted with kind permission from Plan International UK
© 2023 Plan International UK

www.plan-uk.org

Research finds that 97% of women in the UK have been sexually harassed

An investigation by UN Women UK found that 97% of women aged 18-24 have been sexually harassed, with a further 96% not reporting those situations because of the belief that it would not change anything.

Yesterday (10 March), a police officer was arrested in connection to the disappearance of Sarah Everard, a woman who was walking home in the Clapham Common area of London. This news has rippled across the country, resonating with the darkest fears of women who are walking home at night.

Claire Barnett, executive director of UN Women UK, said: 'This is a human rights crisis. It's just not enough for us to keep saying "this is too difficult a problem for us to solve" – it needs addressing now.'

It seems that almost every young woman in the UK has experienced sexual harassment. This figure is completely unsurprising to women who have grown up in the UK. It is common for friends to share traumatic experiences over WhatsApp, to call one another while walking home and to be hesitant in rejecting men who could turn out to be irrationally angry. For women, street harassment is a sobering part of navigating their daily lives.

To be visible at all, is to be targeted.

There seems to be no choice that can avert this kind of horrific experience. Sarah Everard was wearing bright clothes, walking on well-lit residential roads, and in communication with her partner.

A YouGov survey carried out by UN Women UK found that only 4% of women report incidents of sexual harassment, while an overwhelming 96% remain dubious about the UK authorities' capacity to handle an incident like this. Around 45% of the women who would not report sexual harassment in the UK say that it is because nothing would really change.

The dominant stat across media outlets today is that 97% of women aged 18-24 have experienced sexual harassment. This is because the number appears impossibly high to those who have grown up without the experience of sexual harassment as part of their existence.

Researchers further reveal that people who were groped, followed and pressured into sexual activity did not find their experience to be 'serious enough' to report.

'Conventionally attractive' women are more likely to be believed

When it comes to reporting, separate research by the University of Washington found that 'conventionally attractive' women are more likely to be believed. This creates a further divide between the experiences of women who report their sexual harassment, with some being perceived as more valid than others.

Women outside of strict social norms are more likely to be perceived as unharmed by harassment, which means their reports are taken less seriously and can even impact how sexual offenders are sentenced. This includes race, with white women being the expected victim of sexual harassment by a majority of the 4,000 people involved in this research.

When a woman is perceived to be an unlikely victim, sentencing can be less strict for her attacker.

Senior author and UW psychology professor Cheryl Kaiser explained: 'When you make a perception of harassment, you also make a connection to womanhood, but the way we understand womanhood is very narrowly defined.

'So for anyone who falls outside of that definition, it makes it hard to make that connection to harassment.'

In the UN women UK data, 80% of all women said they had been sexually harassed in public spaces in the UK. This experience of sexual harassment appears to be a universal trait of womanhood across the country.

What about street harassment of underage girls?

These findings, and the fact of a police officer being allegedly responsible for the brutal murder of a woman, increase pressure on the Government to create functional interventions for gender-based violence within the UK.

A group of schoolgirls have been campaigning to make street harassment illegal, via the grassroots organisation Our Streets Now.

They found that 72% of pupils who did report public sexual harassment described receiving a negative response from their school, with the majority of participants stating that no real action was taken, while a further 47% didn't report incidents because they were afraid of not being believed or taken seriously.

Some incidents happen in taxis, leaving women and girls highly vulnerable to assault.

A 14 year old student from Essex, Anya, commented: 'Since I was 11 years old I have avoided walking home alone from the bus stop, especially when coming home from school in my uniform.

'Along with the majority of my friends, I have experienced public sexual harassment on multiple occasions. Yet we've never been taught about it.'

7 October 2022

The above information is reprinted with kind permission from Open Access Government
© 2023 Adjacent Digital Politics LTD

www.openaccessgovernment.org

'They're desperate to be accepted': How boys as young as 14 are sucked into the world of incels

A recent report concluded the incel community is 'waging a war' on women and poses a danger to other young men, but are there warning signs when boys are headed down this path?

By Natalie Gil

Derek* had never had a proper conversation with a woman in real life beyond simple exchanges. He didn't have any friends, he had been bullied at school, and now as an adult he was unemployed. He had always felt like he was on the outside of life, looking in.

'He never felt a part of mainstream society and always felt there was something inherently wrong for him,' says journalist Ben Zand, who met Derek, as part of a new Channel 4 documentary, and many others like him who belong to the incel – involuntarily celibate – community in the UK.

There are unifying themes between many of the men finding solace in the incel space, says Zand. They had troubled childhoods, were picked on in their younger years, and became isolated from a young age.

'They [are] desperate for a community, a place to be accepted and a place to feel at home, but sadly found that in the worst place possible, forums that made them lose all hope, hate themselves and blame women for their issues.'

Perhaps most alarming is the age at which boys often fall into this world, explains Maeve Park, an incel researcher from Groundswell Project UK, which is dedicated to building empathy in communities. The extreme misogynist incels Park has seen range from as young as 14 to about 25.

These teenagers and young men tend to have low self-esteem. 'As a society, we've focused a lot on young girls' self-esteem and body image, but we haven't done that with boys as much. So there are many guys who have issues with their height, which I see most frequently, weight, ethnicity, race, mental health issues, their autism, and they have no real places to talk about it freely.'

The incel movement is an online subculture, characterised by extreme misogyny and feelings of sexual frustration with women (and men seen as more sexually successful). '[They] subscribe to an ideological worldview called the blackpill, in which the world is hierarchical and is based solely on appearance, due to the influence of feminism, women being more independent and only picking the very physically attractive men,' explains Park.

In this worldview, all happiness is derived from sexual and romantic fulfilment, so incels believe they will never have a chance at real happiness. 'This creates paranoia, resentment, rage, envy, depression and general hostility as well as alienation and a disinterest in taking part in real life,' Park explains. The incel movement emerged into the mainstream just eight years ago following a mass shooting in California, US, when Elliot Rodger, 22, killed six people, then himself. Rodger left behind a manifesto detailing his hate-filled worldview and membership of the incel movement. Since then its ideas have taken hold quickly on both sides of the Atlantic.

For clarity, not all incels are misogynists and not all misogynist incels are physically violent. While numerous perpetrators of mass shootings are known to have been active in misogynist incel communities, the number of misogynist incels who become violent extremists is relatively low. However, the malignant content and ideas they share are creating an enabling environment in which increasingly dangerous views are encouraged among young men.

The problem is so extreme that a recent report on *The Incelosphere* by the non-profit Centre for Countering Digital Hate (CCDH) concluded the community is 'waging a war' on women, and poses a danger to other young men and an emerging threat to children. Out of almost 1.2 million posts on leading incel forums made over an 18-month period, rape was mentioned every 29 minutes, a fifth contained misogynistic, racist, anti-Semitic, or anti-LGBTQ+ language, and posts mentioning mass murders increased by 59 per cent over the past year.

Now, these extreme ideas are not only found in the internet's darkest corners but on more mainstream platforms too, says Dr Lewys Brace, a senior lecturer at Exeter University specialising in online extremist radicalisation. 'Although the dedicated incel forums very much act as the hubs for this online social community,' he says, 'you find incel content in a whole range of different online spaces, such as YouTube, Discord servers and Telegram channels.'

As these ideas spread, are there pathways to becoming radicalised that people should be aware of? 'You'll typically start to see them receding away from social interactions, spending a lot of time online, and becoming withdrawn,' explains Tim Squirrell, from the Institute for Strategic Dialogue (IDS), a non-profit dedicated to countering extremism and misinformation.

You may hear them express beliefs about themselves, or women, that are consistent with incel beliefs. '[For example] about the hopelessness of sex or romance for them, and derogatory beliefs about women, particularly with respect to promiscuity.' They may also exhibit low moods and start expressing hostility towards women in their vicinity – female family members, including mothers and sisters, classmates and co-workers, says Park.

Experts fear that for many boys, what begins with feelings of isolation, low self-esteem and a resentment of women risks burgeoning into something more sinister. Those mostly likely to succumb to this worldview are typically 'people who struggle with social interaction and may also have difficulties with their appearance,' says Squirrel. There also appears to be a high rate of self-reported autism spectrum disorder among those who identify as incels, he adds.

Men with mental health issues are disproportionately represented, explains Park. 'Misogynist incels may be dealing with extreme anxiety and depression and may be reluctant to accept therapy, as therapy is ridiculed as unhelpful at best and indoctrinating or insulting at worst, and they are more likely to self medicate.'

Very often, young men won't be seeking out incel content before they're served it by internet algorithms. It starts with them Googling innocent questions, says Park. 'When they're feeling low self-esteem, they go online and look up things like "What do girls like?", and "If you're short, will you ever get a girlfriend?", and they'll come across male supremacist content. That's where they find the Andrew Tates [the influencer whose extreme views have earned him a ban from many online platforms]. This is the first port of call for guys who go online with self-esteem issues.'

How can parents help?

- Persist with difficult conversations. It can be distressing to see a loved one moving towards an extreme system of beliefs, says Squirrel. But there is opportunity. 'You'll likely want to reach out to them and try to dissuade them from those beliefs, and that can be frustrating because it often doesn't work, and you may find that they don't trust you to tell them the truth about the world.'

- Do not debate or judge. Park recommends not debating the issue itself but keeping an open dialogue and trying to see what else is going on in their lives, so you can decipher what is really behind these beliefs. 'Open up conversations about feelings, don't judge and try to see if you can help them mental health-wise,' she says.

- Try to get them out of the house. Try to get them out of the house and socialising so they have more of a life in the offline world – rather than feeling they only exist in these online spaces.

- Fathers have a key role. Park says that fathers need to 'take an active part in their sons' emotional life, especially when they're teenagers. We've noticed that mothers often take a lot of the burden when it comes to the emotional wellbeing of their kids.'

- Be willing to seek external help if needed. This is especially if they've displayed violence or are headed that way. Park suggests contacting Prevent if needed and pointing the individual towards therapy and other mental health services.

The speed with which internet algorithms put misogynist incel content in front of people who weren't even looking for it is concerning, says Dr Brace. 'YouTube will take you from one of [controversial Canadian academic] Jordan Peterson's videos to incel content videos within one or two videos, it's that quick a process.' One study by IDS – which created 10 different accounts simulating boys under 18, boys over 18 and two blank control accounts – found that all accounts were eventually led to videos that were 'antagonistic towards women and feminism'.

Fundamentally, misogynist incel forums offer these boys and men something they often don't have in real life: connection. Park describes them as 'a place where teenagers and younger men can go to talk about their insecurities, loneliness and socialising issues in a way that doesn't feel ostracising or alienating'. This speaks to a need for these conversations so that teenage boys and younger men aren't drawn to these dark and violent spaces, she says.

Brace believes a large number of younger boys who engage with this content will disengage from it after a very short period of time. 'Much like how teenagers go through phases of listening to bad music or making questionable fashion choices, they step away from it as they experience more of life and learn better.'

Park describes visiting these forums as a form of 'psychological self harm', because rather than offering support to each other, commenters generally do the opposite. 'They want to keep going back to get that negative reinforcement that yes, they are too ugly, basically. Then the more they feel alienated from everyone else in their life, the more they feel the only places that will allow them in are these forums. They feel like all their friends are in these forums.'

Others will have grown out of it by the time they approach 30, says Park. 'There's often an age cut-off of around 25-26 of interest, because guys, and people in general, get less energetic when it comes to hate. They often find better coping strategies, they get a job, they start to see things differently and they're less anxious.'

Those who get older and haven't gone on to have those experiences will tend to make particularly belligerent posts and have a 'very nihilistic, suicidal, rage-fuelled outlook', says Brace. 'I think that's why when we see the manifestos of individuals who've gone out to commit attacks because they're the ones who hit that point.' There is a higher risk of suicide among this demographic, Park says. 'It's the only ideology I've come across that has as much of a risk factor for the individuals as it does to others.'

But there is hope – men and boys can reverse their beliefs and reintegrate with the world. Derek was 'the most entrenched in that [incel] community when I met him,' says Zand. 'He had fallen down the rabbit hole and was overcome

with the conspiracies that made him obsessed with looks, height, jaw shape, and have really problematic views of women. But spending time with us, and even getting out into the real world on a night out in Southampton, the grip of inceldom appeared to slip and there was a bit of hope that by engagement and deradicalisation there was a way back from the brink.'

If you care about someone potentially in this situation, or heading down this path, you want to be an anchor to reality who can help prevent them becoming completely unmoored, Squirrel says. 'It's unlikely they'll thank you immediately, and you may have to wait a long time before they're willing to hear you out or be helped out of the space they've found themselves in, but if you remain a constant and stable presence in their life then you have a much greater chance of helping them in the long term.'

*Name has been changed

30 November 2022

The above information is reprinted with kind permission from i News.
© 2023 Associated Newspapers Limited

www.inews.co.uk

The draw of the 'manosphere': understanding Andrew Tate's appeal to lost men

An article from The Conversation.

By Ben Rich, Senior lecturer in History and International Relations, Curtin University & Eva Bujalka, Co-director, Curtin Extremism Research Network (CERN), Curtin University

Mega-influencer Andrew Tate is once again back in the news as he battles charges of organised crime and human trafficking in Romania.

Tate gained infamy last year after being banned on most major social media platforms for promoting a variety of aggressively misogynistic positions designed to stir controversy and draw attention to his brand.

But while widespread public attention was drawn to Tate only recently, his reputation as a thought leader and 'top g' in the online 'manosphere' community has been longstanding.

Indeed, Tate's ability to stoke and exploit the anxieties and grievances driving the manosphere are unprecedented, and have played a key role in him amassing millions of fans and hundreds of millions of dollars.

The lure of the 'manosphere'

The manosphere is an overlapping collection of online men's support communities that have emerged as a response to feminism, female empowerment, and the alienating forces of neoliberalism.

While this is widely understood, a lot less energy has been directed to understanding why and how men are attracted to these extreme communities in the first place.

The manosphere's appeal can be perplexing, particularly for parents, teachers or friends trying to make sense of how the men in their lives suddenly adopt aggressively misogynistic views.

But while the community's content presents deeply concerning perspectives on women, it also offers explanations for, and solutions to, a very real set of issues facing young men.

A tranche of data illustrates these growing challenges. Men are rapidly falling behind in education engagement and outcomes. Rates of young male economic inactivity have risen considerably over the past two decades.

The intimate relations of young men also appear to be in decline. One report suggests rates of sexual activity have dropped by nearly 10% since 2002.

Suicide rates have risen significantly in men in particular over the past decade.

We're also facing a loneliness crisis, which is particularly concentrated in young people and men.

The manosphere appeals to its audience because it speaks to the very real lives of young men under the above factors – romantic rejection, alienation, economic failure, loneliness, and a dim vision of the future.

The major problem lies in its diagnosis of the cause of male disenfranchisement, which fixates on the impacts of feminism. Here it contrasts the growing challenges faced by men with the increasing social, economic and political success experienced by women. This zero-sum claim posits that female empowerment must necessarily equate to male disempowerment, and is evidenced through simplified and pseudoscientific theories of biology and socioeconomics.

For many young men, their introduction to the manosphere begins not with hatred of women, but with a desire to dispel uncertainty about how the world around them works (and crucially, how relationships work).

The foundations of the manosphere may not strictly centre on misogyny, as is popularly imagined, but in young men's search for connection, truth, control and community at a time when all are increasingly ill-defined.

Profiteering off anxiety

Since its inception, the manosphere has been rife with predatory influencers seeking to profit off the anxieties unleashed by this ambiguity.

Driven by a desire to reassert a romantic masculine aesthetic ideal in a world of social media unrealities, members of the manosphere often become willing consumers of a wide variety of products and services to 'solve' their problems. These range from vitamin and gym supplements, personal coaching, self-help courses, and other subscription-based services.

But the influencers aren't just capitalising on a sense of crisis passively – they actively cultivate it, as our research shows.

Figures like Tate, Canadian psychologist Jordan Peterson and 'alpha' strongman Elliott Hulse expend huge amounts of energy and capital fomenting a sense of crisis around these issues, and positioning themselves at the centre. No more clearly was this illustrated than in Tate's 'Hustler's University', which created a series of exclusive chat rooms promising men a solution to their fears and centred on Tate's personage and teachings.

Such communities solidify the claims made by their leaders, creating feedback loops that contribute to a climate of tension and hysteria. Members are actively encouraged to ridicule those who aren't willing to acknowledge the 'feminist conspiracies' that supposedly underpin the social and political world. Non-believers are seen as contemptible, weak and ignorant, dismissed through an ever-growing newspeak lexicon as 'simps', 'cucks' and 'betas'.

The community can also be mobilised to spread the message and brand of the influencer to the wider public, as demonstrated by Tate.

Having successfully isolated and indoctrinated community members, influencers can then rely on them as a persistent source of support and revenue, allowing them to further reinvest and continue this cycle of growth. This suggests a key way to push back on the wider effects of the manosphere is the targeted disruption of such feedback loops and the prevention of future ones emerging.

Empathy, patience and support

Tate and the manosphere didn't manifest spontaneously. They're symptoms of a deeper set of challenges young men are facing.

These problems won't be addressed by simply deplatforming people like Tate. While this may often be necessary in the short term, savvier influencers will inevitably emerge, responding to the same entrenched issues and employing the tactics to greater effect, while avoiding the mistakes of their predecessors.

In confronting the manosphere we need to understand and take seriously its appeal to lost men and the centrality of influencers in this process. We can be as critical of it as we want to be. But we also need to understand what it provides for many: a community and place of belonging, a defined enemy, direction, certainty, solutions to deep and systemic issues and, perhaps most importantly, hope.

We also need to avoid the kneejerk stigmatising and dismissal of people who fall into the manosphere. Simple ostracism tends only to entrench attitudes and reinforce the narratives of persecution spun by Tate and his ilk.

Instead, we need to use empathy, tolerance and patience to support men in ways that lead them away from these unpleasant boroughs of the internet and make them feel connected with wider society.

12 February 2023

THE CONVERSATION

The above information is reprinted with kind permission from The Conversation.
© 2010-2023, The Conversation Trust (UK) Limited

www.theconversation.com

Boys at Yorkshire schools idolising misogynist Andrew Tate warn headteachers as they take drastic action

Schools have warned that pupils will be sent home if they copy Andrew Tate.

By Andrew Robinson

Teachers in Yorkshire have revealed how the views of social media personality Andrew Tate have had a negative effect on pupils' behaviour.

School staff in Yorkshire have warned parents to check their children's use of social media and to challenge any form of 'hate speech'.

Tate, 36, is a former kickboxer who has been banned from various social media channels for 'misogynistic comments' after pulling in millions of followers for his 'ultra-masculine' brand and his extreme views on women. Tate is currently in custody in Romania on suspicion of rape and human trafficking. He has denied the allegations.

The former Big Brother contestant, whose TikTok videos have been viewed billions of times, has previously stated that wives are the property of their husbands and that victims of rape 'bear some responsibility' for their own rape. He is often labelled a misogynist for his views.

Schools across Yorkshire have written to parents to inform them of Tate's online content and to explain why his views need to be challenged. His influence is said to be apparent in boys aged from 12 to 16.

Neil Moules, assistant head at Beckfoot Oakbank in Keighley, told parents in a letter: 'We have become aware of a TikTok personality called Andrew Tate who is becoming increasingly prominent on Social Media. He holds some very extreme views and as a school we want to make parents and carers aware of him in case your child makes comments about him at home.

'The information below should help you understand our level of concern about this as a school and also give you some more support if you enter in to conversations about Andrew Tate with your child.

'Within school this week and last, the Executive Head and the Safeguarding lead have addressed the impact of Tate (on) issues of misogyny and toxic masculinity in separate assemblies. Our bespoke Open Minds curriculum and the Tutor lessons for all years discuss issues of discrimination and hatred towards women.

'Teachers have also been sent the information below to make them aware of Andrew Tate's beliefs and Year Teams are meeting with individual students if class teachers have heard discussion in lessons that are supporting of Andrew Tate's views.'

His letter to parents adds: 'We understand that as teenagers who are developing their views of the world, students may not recognise the extremist nature of these views and are therefore more vulnerable to be influenced by them. We are grateful to be able to work in partnership with families to encourage their children in critical thinking around these issues.'

James Lockwood, headmaster at Woodhouse Grove School, Apperley Bridge, said some pupils were behaving as though they supported Tate's views.

'It has become evident that many young men and boys have not been put off following Tate or being influenced by his negative messages,' he told parents in a letter.

'At Woodhouse Grove, we are cognisant that some students are aware of Tate and the opinions he shares online and that they are beginning to exhibit behaviour that would suggest they support his misogynistic and profoundly anti-social beliefs.'

Mr Lockwood urged parents to monitor internet activity at home as well as have 'open and honest discussions' with their children on these subjects.

He said the school would continue to educate students about the danger of Tate's messages, adding: 'In the meantime, I must caution all parents that the School will be adopting a zero-tolerance approach to students publicly expressing views or outward displays of support [including hand gestures] for Andrew Tate's propaganda. Any students behaving in a manner that the School deems to be in total discord with our welcoming, tolerant and compassionate ethos can expect to be sent home.'

Joanna Whetstone, assistant head at The Hayfield School, Doncaster, sent a similar letter home about Andrew Tate which said: 'His content and posts have been removed and banned from many social media platforms, following a successful campaign by UK-based advocacy group Hope Not Hate. However, the banned material is potentially still accessible by young people with a TikTok account or via an internet search. Our staff are vigilant and will share and respond to concerns they have about students who believe are potentially being influenced by inappropriate and offensive views.'

Ms Whetstone added: 'At a time when so many people think it acceptable to use social media for spreading provocative and inflammatory untruths, it is more important than ever that home and school work in partnership to challenge this and other forms of hate speech. Should you have any concerns about how best to support your child to navigate their way through the world of social media, please do not hesitate to contact me.'

6 March 2023

The above information is reprinted with kind permission from YorkshireLive.
© 2023 a Reach plc subsidiary

www.examinerlive.co.uk

Stopping violence against women starts with learning what misogyny really is

An article from The Conversation.

By Katy Dineen, College Lecturer in Teaching & Learning Enhancement, University College Cork & Maria Moulin-Stożek, University Professor, Jan Długosz University in Częstochowa

It's now over a year since 33-year-old Sarah Everard was kidnapped while she walked home and killed by a police officer in London. Since then, we've also seen the case of Sabina Nessa, a primary school teacher also from London, was also killed by a stranger while walking to meet a friend. And in early 2022 in Tullamore, Ireland, 23-year-old Ashling Murphy was killed when out for a run in a public place in daylight hours.

The problem of violence against women might seem insurmountable. But focusing on education about misogyny may provide a place to start. In particular, it is important to help young people understand what misogyny is, how it affects both women and men, and how it can lead to violence.

Our research on moral education, sex education and violence against women can help spell out the link between misogyny and violence, and how education can address these issues.

According to the philosopher Kate Manne, misogyny is not 'hatred of women'. Instead, it is a set of social rules that enforce a patriarchal society – one where men are dominant and women are subordinate. The essence of misogyny lies in its function, and that function is to keep women down.

Misogyny is deeply rooted in society. Girls are regularly assigned lower social status, while masculinity is associated with power and privilege. In an unequal society it is easier to justify violence committed by the more powerful. Women might be treated with scepticism and not believed, while men might be favoured, and their side of the story deemed more credible.

However, misogyny also affects men. Research suggests that men can suffer from a phenomenon known as 'male discrepancy stress' – feelings of distress when they feel they have failed to conform to masculine gender norms.

Male discrepancy stress might come from the idea of being perceived as weak, dependent or emotional. This distress has been linked to male violence against women. When men feel the effects of misogyny, it can have deadly effects upon women.

Educating people about misogyny and its repercussions could be a start in addressing violence against women.

Building identity

Children try to create their own identity, but this can be undermined by gender-based bullying. For instance, a boy who wants to be a nurse when he grows up might suppress this ambition when confronted by the reactions of other children, and instead focus on a more 'masculine' career.

At school, children could be encouraged to reflect on how gender stereotypes have affected them – and how, in turn, their own behaviour might constrain their classmates.

Reflection on gender stereotypes can be guided through philosophy. The central idea behind philosophy for children is to facilitate autonomous learners by encouraging students to think for themselves. Starting with a reflection on how easy it is to rely on stereotypical thinking about gender, the teacher could query how useful or harmful such thinking might be.

Doing philosophy with children is known to have beneficial outcomes for children.

Another approach could use the history of philosophy as a starting point. Older students could be introduced to the work of Mary Wollstonecraft (1759-1797), the so called 'mother of feminism' and a ferocious critic of stereotypical notions of femininity.

However, philosophers have often questioned whether the mother of feminism was herself a misogynist. Students could look at how Wollstonecraft herself may have perpetuated gender norms by accusing fellow philosopher Edmund Burke of not being masculine enough.

Participatory research methods, where young people actively 'do the research', may be a good way to change perspectives. Two Irish school students, Cormac Harris and Alan O'Sullivan conducted a project on gender bias in the classroom and won top prize at the 32nd European Union Contest for Young Scientists.

Harris and O'Sullivan investigated the prevalence of gender stereotypes in children aged from five to seven. They found that gender stereotyping was particularly prevalent among boys, and that boys are less willing to recognise female ability. To combat gender stereotyping, they have gathered resources to be used by teachers and parents that explicitly target gender bias.

Sex education classes can also provide a venue for students to learn about the importance of caring for the other person in a relationship and focusing on their wellbeing when discussing relationships. By incorporating issues of consent and partner violence, these classes can help to prevent misogyny and promote equality between genders.

This type of teaching could help give students a reflective distance from stereotypes, providing them with mental resources which may help when such stereotypes are used against them. In this way, perhaps, teaching could be used in the combat against gender inequality and male discrepancy stress.

14 March 2022

THE CONVERSATION

The above information is reprinted with kind permission from The Conversation.
© 2010-2023, The Conversation Trust (UK) Limited

www.theconversation.com

Useful Websites/ Further Reading

Useful Websites

www.examinerlive.co.uk

www.familylaw.co.uk

www.globalcitizen.org

www.heraldscotland.com

www.human-rights-channel.coe.int

www.independent.co.uk

www.inews.co.uk

www.ntu.ac.uk

www.openaccessgovernment.org

www.plan-uk.org

www.telegraph.co.uk

www.theconversation.com

www.ukfeminista.org.uk

www.verywellmind.com

www.womankind.org.uk

www.womensaid.org.uk

Where can I find help?

Below are some telephone numbers, email addresses and websites of agencies or charities that can offer support or advice if you, or someone you know, needs it.

Childline
Helpline: 0800 1111
www.childline.org.uk

Men's Advice Line
Telephone: 0808 8010 327
Website: www.mensadviceline.org.uk

Rights of Women
Email: info@row.org.uk
www.rightsofwomen.org.uk

Equality and Human Rights Commission – Sexual Harassment
Equality and Advisory Support Service: Freephone 0808 800 0082
www.equalityhumanrights.com

The Survivors Trust
The Survivors Trust provides confidential information, advice and support for people who have experienced rape and sexual violence.
Telephone: 0808 801 0818
www.thesurvivorstrust.org

Victim Support
Supportline: 08 08 16 89 111
www.victimsupport.org.uk

Women's Aid
Email: helpline@womensaid.org.uk
www.womensaid.org.uk

Further Reading

Pages 12-13: Women's Aid, Hester, M., Walker, S-J., and Williamson, E. (2021) *Gendered experiences of justice and domestic abuse. Evidence for policy and practice.* Bristol: Women's Aid

Glossary

Activism
Campaigning to bring about political or social change.

Baiting
A method of provocation. To intentionally make someone angry by doing or saying things to annoy them.

Banter
An exchange of teasing remarks.

Bullying
A form of aggressive behaviour used to intimidate someone. It can be inflicted both physically and mentally (psychologically).

Digital abuse
Most frequently occurring in teenage relationships, digital abuse involves the use of texting and social networking sites to keep track of, harass, stalk, control, bully or intimidate a partner.

Domestic abuse
Any incident of physical, sexual, emotional or financial abuse that takes place within an intimate partner relationship. Domestic abuse can be perpetrated by a spouse, partner or other family member and occurs regardless of gender, sex, race, class or religion.

Extremism
Extremism refers to beliefs or practices that are seen as radical, and can give rise to militance (e.g. groups justifying their violence on Islamic grounds, such as Al-Qaeda).

Feminism
Advocating women's rights and equality between the sexes.

Gender
Gender refers to socially-constructed roles, learned behaviours and expectations associated with females and males. Gender is more than just biology: it is the understanding we gain from society and those around us of what it means to be a girl/woman or a boy/man.

Gender bias
A preference or prejudice toward one gender over the other. Can be conscious or unconscious.

Gender stereotypes
Simplifying the roles, attributes, and differences between males and females. Gender stereotyping encourages children to behave in ways that are considered most typical of their sex. For example, buying pink toys for girls and blue for boys, or limiting girls to playing with dolls and boys to toy cars.

Harassment
Usually persistent (but not always), a behaviour that is intended to cause distress and offence. It can occur on the school playground, in the workplace and even at home.

Homophobia
Homophobia is the irrational fear or hatred of homosexuality (an aversion towards lesbian, gay or bisexual people). This fear can lead to behaviour that discriminates against LGBT people and consequently advantages heterosexuals. Such discrimination is illegal under the Equality Act (Sexual Orientation) Regulations 2007.

Hypermasculinity
Hypermasculinity refers to stereotypical male behaviour, with an emphasis on physical aggression and strength. Hypermasculine traits include: violence, aggressive sexual behaviour and a derogatory attitude towards women. Viewing material such as pornography, in which these traits are exaggerated, can lead to young men believing they should display these characteristics or behaviours.

Incel
An Incel or, involuntary celebate, is an individual (usually male) who blames women and society on their inability to find a romantic partner.

Misogyny
Misogyny is hatred of, contempt for, or prejudice against women.

Objectify/Objectification
To turn something into an object in relation to sight, touch or another physical sense. To 'objectify' a person means to turn them into an object, meaning that they do not possess the same human rights as another individual. The person objectified is usually dominated by another person, or group of people.

Patriarchy
Patriarchy is a social system in which positions of dominance and privilege are primarily held by men.

Prejudice
Referring to prejudgement – forming an opinion before you are fully aware of the facts.

Rape
Forcing someone to engage in sexual intercourse against their will. Force is not necessarily physical, it could also be emotional or psychological.

Rape culture
An environment or culture that normalises sexual violence, trivialises sexual assault and tolerates sexual harrassment against (mostly) women. Rape culture often blames and shames victims while excusing the perpetrator.

Sexism
Sexism is prejudice or discrimination based on one's sex or gender.

Toxic masculinity
A cultural concept of manliness that glorifies stoicism, strength, virility and dominance, and that is socially maladaptive or harmful to mental health.

Index

A
activism 43
Austen, Jane 10–11

B
baiting 43
banter 23, 31, 43
bullying 5, 41, 43

C
catcalling 32
child marriage 2
child-raising 2

D
digital abuse 43
discrimination 1, 19
domestic abuse 12–13, 43
Domestic Abuse Act 2021 13

E
education
    inequality in 3–4, 8–9
    and sexism 3–7, 17, 41
    see also school
Equality Now 1
everyday sexism 1, 15
extremism 43

F
femicide 3
feminism 35, 38, 41, 43
fetishism 33
flashing 33

G
gender 43
gender bias 43
gender stereotyping 1–3, 5–6, 8–13, 41

H
harassment 43
hate speech 2
homophobia 43
homophobic bullying 5
hypermasculinity 43

I
incel culture 21, 35–37, 43
inclusion 2
inequality 2–4, 13

L
language *see* sexist language
LGBTIQ+ 32

M
manosphere 38–39
maternity pay 2
MeToo movement 28–29
misogynist language 3, 5
misogynoir 19–20
misogyny 13, 18–20, 22–26, 35–41, 43
    definition 5

N
name calling 5
Northanger Abbey 10–11

O
objectification 13, 22, 43

P
patriarchy 43
power, and sexism 1
princessification 8

R
rape 24, 25–26, 31, 36, 40, 43
rape culture 22, 43
relationships, domestic abuse 12–13, 43

S
school, sexism in 3–7, 40
self-esteem 8, 35
sexism
    definition 1–2
    in education 3–7, 17
    in the home 12–13, 17
    in literature 10–11
    reporting 3, 7
    in schools 3–7, 40
    tackling 3
    in the workplace 15–17
sexist language 3, 5, 15, 22
sexist scripts 12–13
sexual harassment 3–4, 28, 32–34
sexualisation, of school uniform 33
social media 15
stereotyping 1–3, 5–6, 8–13, 41
street harassment 14, 17, 26–27, 29–34
structural inequalities 13
suicide 8

T
Tate, Andrew 25, 36, 38–40
toxic masculinity 27, 40, 43
transmisogyny 20

U
United Nations, Sustainable Development Goals 2

V
violence 14

W
Weinstein, Harvey 28
Women's Aid 12–13
workplace sexism 15–17